# Pondering the Meaning of Life

# Pondering the Meaning of Life

*A Skeptic's Thoughts
on Christian Faith,
God, and the Afterlife*

Ian D. H. Smith

RESOURCE *Publications* • Eugene, Oregon

PONDERING THE MEANING OF LIFE
A Skeptic's Thoughts on Christian Faith, God, and the Afterlife

Copyright © 2019 Ian D. H. Smith. All rights reserved. Except for brief quotations in critical publications or reviews, no part of this book may be reproduced in any manner without prior written permission from the publisher. Write: Permissions, Wipf and Stock Publishers, 199 W. 8th Ave., Suite 3, Eugene, OR 97401.

Resource Publications
An Imprint of Wipf and Stock Publishers
199 W. 8th Ave., Suite 3
Eugene, OR 97401

www.wipfandstock.com

PAPERBACK ISBN: 978-1-5326-9156-0
HARDCOVER ISBN: 978-1-5326-9157-7
EBOOK ISBN: 978-1-5326-9158-4

Manufactured in the U.S.A.                  DECEMBER 2, 2019

All biblical quotations are from the New Revised Standard Version Bible, copyright © 1989, Division of Christian Education of the National Council of the Churches of Christ in the United States of America. Used by permission. All rights reserved.

# CONTENTS

Part I—Introduction
    1 The Trout and God | 3
    2 Welcome the Curious | 11

Part II—Christianity Unpacked
    3 Life for the Jews around thirty AD | 27
    4 Jesus the Prophet | 36
    5 Jesus Declared as the Christ | 52
    6 The Quest to Understand | 69

Part III—Thoughts
    7 Thoughts on Religion | 89
    8 Thoughts on Life and Death | 101
    9 Thoughts on God | 111
    10 Final Thoughts | 121

    *Bibliography* | 131

# Part I

## INTRODUCTION

# 1

## THE TROUT AND GOD

Is this as good as it gets? Is there anything else to life? What is the meaning of my life? If you have ever asked yourself questions like these then this book is for you.

In the past most people found answers to these questions within their religion but today many people in the Western world may still live in a nominally Christian culture but find some aspects of the Christian faith difficult to accept. In particular, talk of miracles and supernatural events just do not seem credible. However, those same people might also feel that they would like to find out if there really are any meaningful answers to those questions or if all thoughts around spirituality and religion are for the gullible and are basically delusionary. Of one thing, however, we can all be certain: one day, we will die.

I am not wishing to be morbid or depressing but, although your expectation may be that that day is still far off, it will come. Now, at this very early stage in the book, you may already be concerned that the rest of the book is going to be full of moral guidance and preaching on how you should lead your life in order to prepare for some expected judgement in the afterlife. Rest assured that it is not that kind of book but it is rather more like a self-help book that looks at the evidence, provides information, and

PART I—INTRODUCTION

explores some ideas to help you decide for yourself how to think about your own life and death. For example, you may wish to find the answers to these three questions before that final day gets too near.

- Will your death be the end of you or is there something more?
- Is it credible to have religious belief in the twenty-first century?
- Can there be a deeper meaning to life?

Perhaps it is beyond most of us to even contemplate that we should search for the meaning of life. But what about considering if there is any serious prospect of life after death and, if there is, should we be doing anything to prepare for it? Should we be changing the way we live? Should we go to church occasionally? Or are all religions just for the gullible and those afraid of some divine punishment? Perhaps we could talk to the local priest/iman/rabbi etc. but that conversation feels like it would be way too uncomfortable. Better, therefore, to park those questions for now and wait until we have more time. But even when we do find time it is not obvious where to start as it seems almost impossible to find some impartial advice and information. Any religious organization or minister is, almost by definition, going to promote their own faith as knowing the truth and providing the answers to your questions. All you need to do is believe.

## Avoidance

Have you ever considered how good we are at avoiding doing those awkward tasks that we know we should really do? It is not just a matter of how easily we can decide that it will be tomorrow when we start that diet or enroll at the gym but it is also our unerring ability to find compelling reasons why it is just not the right time to have that embarrassing conversation. We also fill our lives with so many distractions that we sometimes seem not to be able to find the time to think. (Strange then that we can always find time to daydream about what house we would buy when we win the lottery, or to catch up on the latest reality television program.) As for those really heavy questions about the meaning of life or whether there is life after death, well, they are readily banished to the back of the list of things to do.

Many of us nowadays have a reasonable expectation that we will live until our old age. An earlier death from war, famine or disease is not the fate that awaits most of us so perhaps we no longer feel the need to be prepared for an unexpected meeting with the divine. In much of the developed world we have the freedom to choose how we live our lives. We can choose who to marry; we can choose to be open about our sexual orientation; we can choose how to spend our money; we can choose how much to eat and drink. We are free to choose if we believe in a God or not. Perhaps life was actually easier when our religion was mainly decided at birth. As children we would be taken by our parents to their place of worship and be expected to join with them in their faith. Now we have the freedom to choose any religion we wish, or none. This can be a daunting prospect, so far simpler to put off thinking about the subject until we get older.

As we grow into adulthood we all develop egos and actively work to avoid any damage or risk to this precious sense of self. When we were children we accepted that adults knew more than we did and we did not struggle against receiving lessons from them. However, as adults we can feel embarrassed by not knowing what all the others seem to know or not understanding what is expected of us in a given circumstance. This can be a significant barrier to entering any new situation and especially your local place of worship. You may just be curious and interested to know what goes on within the building, but we can all feel uncomfortable even when people are friendly and we are welcomed.

## "God Is Dead"

The German philosopher Friedrich Nietzsche (1844–1900) is credited with the above saying, which has become popular in recent times as more and more people feel that modern scientific explanations of how the world works has made the need for belief in a deity superfluous. Some people may dismiss religious beliefs out of hand but that is the route of the lazy (and the bigoted). My prime interest is to consider and discuss what we can say about the meaning of life (if anything). However, we have to acknowledge that religious faith provides meaning for the lives of many people across the globe and those religions claim to know the truth about God, what awaits us after death, and how we should conduct our lives here on earth if we are to reap rewards in the afterlife. It would therefore be foolish to just ignore what people have believed for generations and assume that we know better. Not only that but, I would suggest, it is disrespectful.

Religious faith has, for thousands of years, provided the basis of cultures and held together societies by means of a shared set of beliefs and understanding of how life is to be lived and what is to be expected after death. No matter how awful the actual experience of life, the priests would declare that the suffering should be endured for the sake of a better deal during the eternity to come. If our ponderings are to be credible then we have to make the effort of understanding religious beliefs.

*Can religion still hold the key to unlocking the mystery of the meaning of life to us in the twenty-first century?*

That question is not answered by just cataloguing the beliefs and teachings of a religion. Before we can decide if those beliefs are credible it is necessary to understand how those beliefs came into being and how they, and the associated teachings, have evolved over the centuries. We need to dig down and uncover the origins of the religion and determine the verifiable historical roots. Only once we truly understand how religious beliefs arose can we be in a position to determine which, if any, could be considered to be credible. Thus we have some hard work to do.

You may be reading this but have no real interest in a religion that appears illogical and contrary to twenty-first-century scientific understandings of how things work. The religious folk you encounter are either deaf to rational argument or so bigoted that it is best to avoid any discussion. Perhaps you are the exact opposite and have a strong personal faith that you may accept cannot be scientifically analyzed yet is nonetheless very real to you. Others can have just a strong faith that there is no such thing as God; God is dead and science has looked for and failed to find any evidence of a human soul. I hope that the very fact that you have read this far indicates that you have some curiosity and interest in exploring if there is any other way to think about religion and the meaning of life. I should give a general health warning at this point. Most of you will, I hope, find your preconceptions challenged but some may find what I say disrespectful if not downright insulting. Trust me in that I have no desire to insult anyone's beliefs but only to open up other patterns of thought that you may find rewarding. I totally respect your right to disagree with what I may suggest and dismiss me as misguided. The choice is yours and yours alone.

Perhaps before we go any further I should say something about the somewhat weird title of this chapter. In 2012 a typically British film was released called *Quartet*, about a retirement home primarily for those from the music industry and starring Dame Maggie Smith, Tom Courtney, Pauline Collins, and Billy Connolly (later Sir Billy Connolly). It was directed by the American Dustin Hoffman. In an interview to promote the film Billy Connolly is reported as saying, "I've absolutely no idea if God exists. It seems unlikely to me, but then does a trout know that I exist?" I guess Billy said that partly in jest, but maybe there is more to it that just an amusing quote intended to get publicity for a film. What if we likened our attempts to talk about a God who is so utterly different from ourselves to be beyond the capability of human language to describe, to the trout's attempt to talk about us by blowing bubbles? Both the trout and we have a challenging task ahead.

## Help Is at Hand

This book provides some help in tackling this challenging task because, when we do find time to do some thinking, it can seem scary and all rather too difficult to do by ourselves. The irony is that the people who try to talk to you about God and religion are precisely the type of people you would cross the road to avoid. The aim of this book is to provide a relatively painless start to help you think about what may or may not be believable around those big questions. It will not tell you what to believe—there are far too many people already more than willing to do that—and it will be up to you to decide if you have enough information to come to a conclusion or if you need to find out more. You may well decide that you need to find out more, but decide to put that off until you have more time. It may frustrate you that I won't tell you what is correct and what is not but expect you to decide for yourself helped by the information in this book. It is the nature of this area of our lives that there is so much preached and written yet it is ultimately up to each of us to come to our own conclusions. One key piece of advice is to beware of those who are certain, whether they are certain that there definitely is a basis for believing in God and religion or equally certain that any thoughts of God are delusionary.

My contention is that this is not a religious book in that it does not set out to foster belief in any religious system. However, as previously discussed, for many people the key to the meaning of their lives is their religious faith, so no book looking at the meaning of life can avoid including a look at religion. Although I have tried to avoid pushing any one belief system or set of cultural values, I cannot escape the fact that I come from a Western, Christian background and this has inevitably influenced all my thoughts and actions. I have looked at the development and basis of Christianity in particular, not because I wish to emphasize Christianity more than other religions but, to be honest, because that was the easiest approach for me.

This book provides the knowledge that will allow everyone to think for themselves about what is right for them personally regarding faith and their take on the meaning of life. Although that means I will discuss both religion and God, I do reiterate that this is not a religious book. There will be no preaching, no saying what God wants you to do, no saying what you should or should not do with your lives in order to guarantee that you will have some sort of glorious afterlife. My intention is also to make this a book that is readable by all and not just those who are knowledgeable about religion and/or theological theories. As far as possible I will avoid jargon and not get involved in too much detail or in complicated arguments. I shall also keep it short. I hope that I present the information in a way that treats the reader as intelligent without assuming any prior knowledge other than some very basic understanding of Christianity that may, for instance, be taught in first school. I have strived to avoid bias towards or against any religion or belief in God and an afterlife. I do, however, repeat my warning that none of us can ever mentally separate ourselves from our cultural background and our religious prejudices and this prevents any truly unbiased analysis. Once you have read this book it is my hope that you will be able to make your own choices, and I would be completely happy for you not to follow what I believe. This is not an academic textbook. You will not find lists of cross-references and original research from primary sources. You may not even find many original thoughts and ideas as I have shamelessly built upon the work of others. What I hope you will find is a practical and commonsense approach to thoughts about God, the afterlife, and religion but I urge you to be careful and check anything I may say before accepting it as a fact.

Although the aim of this book is to help you work out some answers for yourself, before the end of the book I will provide my own attempts to answer those three questions that were posed earlier. The guiding principle I have used during my pondering has been, "Does this make sense to me and does it seem reasonable?" Often I have found that you just have to have confidence in your own judgement or you soon get buried under the weight of advice from well-meaning colleagues and experts. Thus in considering what actually took place in the distant past I considered that the laws of nature, and the behavior of humans, worked then as they do now. I also consider the evidence to decide if we should consign to the past ideas that gods once walked upon the earth and that talk of superhuman abilities should be left to the comic books. Death

PART I—INTRODUCTION

comes to us all and many people may not be frightened by the prospect of being dead but are anxious about the process of dying. I expect we have all known people who have had a bad death in that their last few months were undignified or they suffered pain. I cannot help you with the dying apart from reducing the anxiety of what is to follow. As we get older it is natural to think more about what is to come but few go to their death confident of what follows.

# 2

## WELCOME THE CURIOUS

It seems that over the past two centuries or so there have been tremendous advances in almost every field of human endeavor. Advances in science and technology have allowed us to understand how and why things work as they do. We can send people into space and use probes to explore far beyond our own solar system. We now understand how our actions influence the environment so we have choices to make about what we are going to do if we wish to avoid irreversible changes. We have the ability to use technology to free people from both hard and dangerous work and also from boring, repetitive tasks. We can even use technology to design better technology. Science has provided an understanding of how we evolved over the millennia to become the human animals we are today. We can catalogue how we are killing other species and again we have choices to make. We can clone and manipulate domesticated animals to better serve our desire to eat meat and dairy products whilst we are also dramatically increasing the yield of our crops. As the human population goes on expanding we have the knowledge and capability to keep expanding the food supply to keep pace, and to provide assistance in times of natural disasters, so that famines today are normally the result of human wars or indifference.

# PART I—INTRODUCTION

Advances in medicine allow us to explain the factors that influence our health. People are now far more aware how diet, exercise, and lifestyle choices will impact our physical health and thus determine our chances of living to an active old age. Despite this many of us eat too much, drink too much alcohol, or indulge in recreational drugs and hope that any detrimental impact on our health can be reversed by the doctors. Other factors, including hygiene and disease control, are improving in nearly every corner of the planet.

Advances in psychology provide an understanding of how we behave as individuals and as groups. We can determine the factors that drive our ambitions, provide the motivation to change things and to buy one particular car as opposed to another. Psychiatrists can help mental illnesses that were previously blamed on possession by demons. Chemical imbalances in the brain can be reversed by modern drugs and therapy can overcome many behavioral disorders.

## Spirituality/Faith

So why then does one area of human activity seem to have missed out in the general advancement of human knowledge and capability? Our attitudes and approaches to faith and religion seem to be stuck in the distant past and many of our religious practices would be recognizable to someone from five hundred years ago. Okay, there have been changes in some religions regarding aspects such as participation by women, but the rate of change is painfully slow. I know there are earnest academics beavering away in universities and theological colleges but they have had minimal impact on the general population compared to advances in the other areas of our lives as outlined above. The daily news we hear is often dominated by acts of war and aggression motivated by religious fanaticism. Muslims kill other Muslims, Christians kill other Christians, Sikhs battle Hindus and extremists in nearly every religion appear to believe they have a divine duty to attack anybody who has a different faith. Crazy! Perhaps the world would be a much better and happier place if we could get rid of religion altogether.

But do we need to do anything? Perhaps the days of religious beliefs are naturally coming to an end as our understanding in all the other areas allows us to live contentedly without the need for a God. In the Western world there has been a significant decline in the number of people who actively participate in religious practices and it can be expected that this trend will continue if nothing is done to change things. However, there does seem to be a general agreement that something is missing in society and there is a need to find a replacement for the role once undertaken by religion.

## The Study of God

If we are to consider if there is any meaning to our lives we will need to ponder the existence, or not, of a God who is watching over us. The study of God is called theology and those that do it are called theologians. In the cult science fiction comedy written by Douglas Adams, *The Hitchhiker's Guide to the Galaxy*, we meet Marvin, the depressed robot, who moans that he has a brain "the size of a planet" but is usually assigned menial tasks such as picking up litter. Sometimes it feels that you also need a brain the size of a planet to enter the world of theology and this can induce a significant inferiority complex in the rest of us. Perhaps it is time to be brave (or just deluded) and charge into the discussion in the hope that some fresh air will allow the general public to gain access to the world of theology.

Over the generations there have been, and there are still today, many brilliant theologians. Their deliberations have resulted in substantial works leading to the formulation of religious dogma that balance often contradictory beliefs with great skill and care. However, many of their books are written for fellow theologians and academics and hence, to put it mildly, tend to be a very hard read for the average interested member of the public. They use a language and jargon that requires a layperson to always have at hand a dictionary of religious terms (or access to Google). One

## PART I — INTRODUCTION

difficulty I often found was that by the time I had worked my way through the detailed analysis presented in support of the author's view I had lost sight of the underlying fundamental truth being debated. This, however, is the world that the academic must inhabit. Every point must be proven; every source of evidence has to be traced back to its origins. If this rigorous discipline is not followed then the work would quickly be dismissed within academic circles. The great gift that academics freely give to the world is the improved understanding of their subject. However, this improved understanding is not always easily accessible to those of us outside of the academic world. It can take many years for the academic world to come to a consensus, so at any one time there can be many different theories regarding the particular aspect being studied. Within Christian theology there are a huge number of very worthy studies and books dedicated to the New Testament that are invaluable in providing a new understanding of the life and teachings of Jesus together with the basis of the Christian faith. In addition to the works of academics there are many books written by priests and devout members of a particular religion but, no matter how hard the author may try, their own beliefs color everything they write. I sometimes find myself getting frustrated upon reading books that include statements such as "God wants us to . . ." and "In order for you to be guaranteed a place in heaven you must . . ." How can anyone possibly know that for certain, and why should I just accept that to be the truth? I fully accept that the author is sincere and they truly believe what they are saying is the truth but why should I believe them and not someone else who is equally sincere but believes something totally different to be the truth?

To be fair, there are many interesting and readable books available and I have included a list of some of those that I found particularly useful within the bibliography. The approach I have taken is to pick and compare ideas and concepts from the various authors and lecturers to determine what seems to make sense. I still remember the great relief I felt when I realized that it was not necessary to accept that miraculous events that were said to have happened in the past were historically accurate. There is a substantial body of Christians who take a liberal approach to their theology and seem willing to embrace doubts regarding some traditional beliefs. However, at times it seems as though these ideas are too dangerous to be brought to the attention of the general church-going public as it may rock the established perception of religious life and faith.

I suggest, however, there is a need to go even further and question some of the traditional foundations of religion to see if there is a way of thinking that may be less comforting to some, but may provide many people with a new way of thinking about life and death. This is not a task for an ordained minister or someone committed to a faith (be that a faith in a God or a faith that there is no God). It is therefore with much trepidation that I offer my own thoughts. I believe you need to stand back occasionally from all the information that is being presented and just ask yourself if it feels right. That is what I have attempted to do in the following pages. I anticipate that some readers will conclude that I do not fully appreciate nor understand many aspects and have hence oversimplified a complex subject. Others may find they are upset by my approach and feel that I am being disrespectful to their deeply held beliefs.

Perhaps before I get worried about being ridiculed for my views I need to get that fear into perspective and consider what has happened to theologians in the past. For example, Servetus was a Spanish theologian who developed a particular view of God and the Christian faith for which I have much sympathy. While visiting Geneva, Servetus was arrested for his views and, on the twenty-seventh of October 1553, he was burned at the stake just outside the city. In more recent times Dietrich Bonhoeffer, one of the foremost theologians of the twentieth century, was hanged for his opposition to the evil of Nazism. In the light of their fates I should not be too concerned about the possibility of a few dismissive or critical reviews.

As already mentioned, I will use Christianity as an example of a major religion and dig down to ascertain what it is that provides

PART I—INTRODUCTION

the bedrock of the faith. In doing so it is not my intention to either promote Christianity or attack Christianity. It would be ideal if I could look at a whole range of different religious traditions but that would be a very large exercise and an equally large book. Having been raised and living in Western Europe, I know more about Christian culture and religious practices than any other religion but I have no reason to expect that the broad conclusions would be very different for other religions.

You may assume that someone who says that they are a Christian is someone who believes in the teachings of Jesus but that is not so clear if you look at what the Christian church actually preaches. If you go to a Christian church service it is likely that at some point in the proceedings the whole congregation will stand and declare what they believe by reciting one of the creeds. One of the most widely used is the 1662 text of the Apostles' Creed as below (or a more modern translation):

> I believe in God the Father Almighty, Maker of heaven and earth: And in Jesus Christ his only Son, our Lord, Who was conceived by the Holy Ghost, Born of the Virgin Mary, Suffered under Pontius Pilate, Was crucified, died, and was buried, He descended into hell; Third day he rose again from the dead, He ascended into Heaven, And sitteth on the right hand of God the Father Almighty; From thence he shall come to judge the quick and the dead. I believe in the Holy Ghost, the holy Catholick Church; The communion of Saints; The forgiveness of sins; The resurrection of the body, And the Life everlasting. Amen.[1]

Thus the congregation reaffirms their belief in God, Jesus and the Holy Ghost/Spirit (the Trinity) along with the church, saints, forgiveness, resurrection, and life everlasting. About Jesus they reaffirm their belief in his birth by a virgin, his crucifixion, his descent and ascension, and his second coming as a judge. However, there is absolutely no mention at all about what he did and taught. How can that be? We need to understand what role Jesus has in

1. Cranmer, *Book of Common Prayer*.

Christianity and why the creed has been developed to say what it says. Only then can we be in a position to make a valid assessment over the claims made by the Christian church and, by some general extrapolation, the claims made by other religions.

If we do not make the effort to understand what religious belief is, and where that belief has come from, we are open to the charge of dismissing religion and quoting the saying "God is dead" without any justification. Hence I will repeat, yet again, that this is not intended to be a religious book but I believe we need to understand what religious faith is based on. Is there a solid foundation to the faith that can make it credible?

It is often said that humankind needed to invent gods in order to allow them to make sense of the often terrifying and unpredictable world around them with multiple diseases and natural disasters, including devastating storms and earthquakes. Whether this is true or not, there does also seem to be evidence of a worldwide human experience of something beyond the knowable. However, although the study of when and why humans began to come to believe in various deities may well prove interesting, it does not form part of this book. Many cultures developed a belief in many gods. This is called polytheism. Typically these religions include a belief in other malevolent demonic and ghostly forces in addition to the gods. Sometimes there is just one supreme God with other gods being subservient or representing the various aspects and tasks of the supreme God. For example in ancient Egypt each of the various gods and goddesses represented one or more aspect of the world. Ra was the sun god, Nut was the goddess of the sky, Ptah was the creator god, Isis was the goddess of funeral rites, etc. In Greece the various gods ruled various aspects of the natural world and human endeavor. Zeus was the supreme God whilst his brother Poseidon was the god of the sea and earthquakes, and his other brother Hades ruled the underworld and the dead. Aphrodite was the goddess of love; Apollo was god of many aspects including the sun, music and dance; Dionysus was the god of wine and vegetation, etc.

PART I—INTRODUCTION

In part II I look in more detail at the rise and development of Christianity as an example of a major religion. It is beyond the scope of this book to look in detail at all of the world's major religions but you may wish to carry out a similar exercise with any religion of your choice. In the following few pages I give a (very) brief picture of some religions before the birth of Jesus of Nazareth, my purpose being to give some idea of the background to religious beliefs that gave life meaning and influenced every aspect of life in those ancient days.

## Mithraism

In the past there have been numerous religious cults but I will outline just the one known as Mithraism. The worship of the Indo-Persian god Mithra dates back thousands of years. The god was known as Mitra in the Indian Vedic religion and was essentially a sun god as was the Persian version, known as Mithra. Worshipping Mithra provided freedom from sin and disease and was the pathway to spiritual purity.

Over the millennia there was much development in the worship of this sun god and there are at least three variants:

- Mitra, the Vedic god.
- Mithra, the Persian deity.
- Mithras, within the Greco-Roman world.

Mithra's mother was Anahita, which means pure/untainted, and she has been identified with the virgin goddess Artimis, an Indo-Iranian goddess of antiquity. Following the military campaigns of Alexander the Great in the fourth century BC, Mithra became a favored deity throughout Asia Minor. Mithraism began to be absorbed by the Romans during military campaigns around 70 BC and spread throughout the Roman Empire.

Modern-day studies of Mithraism within the Greco-Roman world have been hampered by centuries of biased reports by Christian historians but many have concluded that Mithra was born on the twenty-fifth of December of the virgin Anahita, became a great teacher and master, had twelve companions, performed miracles, sacrificed himself for world peace, and ascended into heaven. Does that sound like a familiar story?

## Rome

Rome was founded in approximately 750 BC by Romulus. There were many legends surrounding him, some of which may also seem familiar. The story of his birth, for instance, has King Amulius forcing his niece Rhea Silvia into a lifetime of virginity as a vestal priestess, but she gives birth to twin boys (Remus and Romulus). Her uncle orders their death and a servant is given the task of killing them, but instead he places them in a basket and leaves it on the banks of the River Tiber, which rises in flood and carries the twins downstream where they are saved. At the end of his life, the legend has Romulus disappearing in a storm or whirlwind. The senate declared that Romulus was not dead but had been seen rising up to heaven and had been transformed into a higher being.

The Romans absorbed many of the gods of other peoples and especially the Greek gods, whom they renamed. Hence Zeus became Jupiter, Poseidon became Neptune, Hades became Pluto, Aphrodite became Venus, and Dionysus became Bacchus, while Apollo remained Apollo. By the start of the first century AD Augustus was the Roman emperor. New gods were continually being brought to Rome from various parts of the empire, causing many new religious cults to be established. Augustus created a tradition of divine rulers that placed emperors among these gods of the Roman state. Augustus ruled until his death in 14 AD, when he was succeeded by his stepson Tiberius, who, by definition, was the stepson of a god. However, the term "son of a god" was used for all emperors without regard to whether this was biologically correct.

## Origins of Judaism

In order to make sense of most of the major world religions it is necessary to have some basic understanding of the religion of the Jews, i.e., Judaism.

PART I — INTRODUCTION

The history of the Jews and their religion are inseparable. The story starts about four thousand years ago in the Bronze Age when there was a shepherd called Abram, who lived in what is now Iraq. Remember that this was a time when there was widespread worship of many gods but Abram was a deeply religious man who developed an intense belief in one supreme God. This God made Abram a promise that, if he obeys everything that God asks, he will have numerous descendants and land. Abram faithfully does as God asks and so, as a sign of their special relationship, God changes Abram's name to Abraham. Abraham and his wife, Sarah, are getting on in age before the birth of their first child, a son named Isaac. However, in order to test Abraham's obedience God orders him to sacrifice Isaac and astonishingly Abraham obeys and takes his son up into the mountains to be sacrificed. At the very last minute God relents and provides a sheep as an alternative sacrifice.

Over the following centuries the Jewish people suffer many hardships so that, approximately a thousand years after the time of Abraham, they were living as slaves in Egypt with the prophet Moses as their leader. Moses, with the help and guidance of God, led the Jews out of Egypt to the land that God had promised Abraham. When they had reached Mount Sinai Moses went up the mountain, where God spoke to him and made a new deal with the Jews (known as a covenant) in which God promised to look after the Jews and they promised to obey the teachings of God. These teachings were set down in a set of rules known as the Law. Although the most famous of these are the Ten Commandments, there are in fact 613 such rules covering every aspect of life. God commanded Moses to have built an ark to house the tablets on which were written the commandments, and is hence known as the Ark of the Covenant. This ark was a wooded box covered inside and out with gold and carried on two poles again made of wood covered in gold and thus the ark was carried wherever the Jews went.

In about 1000 BC the Jews had a new king named David, who is remembered as a great King by the Jewish people. David established Jerusalem as his capital city and moved the Ark of the

Covenant there so that Jerusalem also became the religious center for the Jews. David's son and successor, Solomon, built a great temple to house the ark and so the temple became the focal point of worship for all the Jews and was recognized as the most holy place where the actual presence of God could be felt. However, in about 600 BC the Babylonians sacked the temple and the Ark of the Covenant was lost forever. Many Jews were sent into exile and, although they were soon allowed to return home, many stayed in foreign lands, hence the tradition of Jews living away from Israel (known as the Diaspora) was established.

This brings to an end the brief look at religions prior to the time of Jesus. In part II we look in more detail at Judaism and Jewish life at the time of Jesus.

## Approach

In various places during the foregoing I have mentioned aspects of the approach and methods I shall be using and I now wish to bring them all together:

1. Common sense: Perhaps the most important, but subjective, aspect is the application of common sense. I do appreciate that what is obviously common sense for me is just as obviously nonsense to someone else.

2. Consistency: Humans were just as intelligent in the past as they are now and the laws of nature applied in the past just as they do now (even though they may have not been understood at the time). Likewise, human nature, both the good and the bad aspects, has not altered significantly. I must, however, add one caveat at this point as some will argue that God can decide to intervene and change the laws of nature or human behavior. Indeed these interventions, such as demonstrated in miracles, may be seen by some as proof that God exists.

3. The work of others: I have already admitted that I have pieced together various ideas and thoughts harvested from various

PART I—INTRODUCTION

books and lectures. I do not consider this to be exceptional as most of human progress and ideas are built on the shoulders of those who have gone before.

4. Possibilities and probabilities: What we are left with is a range of possibilities and a disappointing lack of certainty. I will try and give some guidance and share my own thoughts but the rest is up to you to continue and find your own path through life. If you feel that this is going to be unsettling then maybe this book is not for you and you will be more comfortable with a preacher who will assure you that he/she knows the way and the truth.

The above is the approach I have taken in writing this book but perhaps it is also worth saying a few words on the approach you may like to take when you read this book. Although I have strived to keep things straightforward there is no doubt that theological ideas can seem complicated and it is easy to despair and think that it is going to be too difficult to understand what is being said. However, I would urge you to keep in mind that what is most important is to get a feel for the big picture and not get stuck in the detail. Theologians seem to love to make simple concepts complex. Therefore when a particular point seems obscure perhaps you may wish to pass over that particular point and carry on regardless. You can always come back later to try and understand the details once you have the major concepts clear in your mind.

The rest of this book is divided into two further parts: part II, Christianity Unpacked; part III, Thoughts.

Part II looks at Christianity and attempts to understand the historical events surrounding Jesus of Nazareth and the subsequent development of the Christian faith. At this point it may be wise to pause and consider how incredibly difficult it is to reconstruct what actually happened two thousand years ago. It certainly must be far more difficult than to reconstruct what happened just over one hundred years ago where we have access to photographs and written reports from the time. Douglas Smith has written a very well-researched book about Rasputin,[2] the Russian holy man who lived just over one hundred years ago and who was a favorite of the Tsar Nickolas and Tsarina Alexandra of Russia. Personally I found the book hard going, with all the unfamiliar Russian names and words, but it does demonstrate that nearly everything I thought I knew about Rasputin was incorrect. Douglas Smith studied all the records written at the time, including writings by Rasputin himself, to show that, although Rasputin did have many weaknesses, his subsequent reputation as a drunken womanizer who had an unacceptable relationship and hold on the royal family were lies made up by those establishment figures he had upset. Stories about his extraordinary powers and healing abilities were also gross exaggerations.

How much more difficult then must it be to reach back, not just one hundred years, but two thousand years to learn the truth behind the stories surrounding Jesus of Nazareth. My plea to you is to put aside all you think you know about Jesus and just read part II as non-judgmentally as you can. I have attempted to write the story of Christianity in a chronological order that may be difficult to grasp as all the material that you may have read previously has probably been written from the viewpoint of looking back after deciding that Jesus was a special being.

*Remember that much of the story of Jesus of Nazareth is similar to other ancient stories and perhaps it is not as unique as many may wish to believe.*

In part III I provide a series of thoughts on various aspects that may help when pondering the meaning of our lives. I start by returning to religion and, after discussing the events that gave rise to the Christian faith, discuss if religion can bring anything positive to our lives today and, if so, what and how. I will share some thoughts that may help you choose how to proceed. I then look at the possibility of a continuing existence after our death. Again, what is the evidence one way or the other? Are there alternative

2. Smith, *Rasputin*.

## PART I—INTRODUCTION

ways we can approach the whole issue? How can we determine if God exists or not? If God does exist, how can we get to know what God is like? I have to accept the fact that many people have gone before with the same questions but if there are definite, verifiable answers to these questions then they should be well known and accepted. Maybe there is a different way of tackling the questions by considering what else we know that may provide some other possibilities. Finally (and at last) I attempt to answer those three questions I posed at the beginning of this book and leave you with some thoughts that may help you in reaching a meaning for your own life.

So for the curious, welcome and please leave any preconceptions behind.

(I should mention that you are free to decide to skip part II and read part III before deciding if you want to return to part II and put the effort into understanding the foundations of Christianity. However, I personally believe that the logical sequence is to first understand a religion before deciding on the credibility, or not, of that religion.)

## Part II

# CHRISTIANITY UNPACKED

# 3

## LIFE FOR THE JEWS AROUND THIRTY AD

My purpose in part II is to get under the skin of the Christian faith so that we can understand where it came from and why it is what it is today. Why do Christians recite the creed that I quoted earlier? Where did that come from and what does it mean? Are there any real solid foundations to the faith or is it just another ancient story like many myths and legends?

We begin the story of Christianity by considering what life was like for the average Jew living in the first century AD and, in particular, around 30 AD, when Jesus of Nazareth began his mission. Life in Roman occupied Israel for the average Jew was hard—very hard. The economy of first-century Israel was based on three key industries: agriculture, large government building projects, and trade around the Mediterranean. The majority of the people were poor rural peasants and life was exceedingly tough for most. The Roman government required heavy taxation of its people and assigned the job of tax collector to the individual who would do the job for the lowest pay, so he, in order to make a decent living, would collect additional taxes for himself.

PART II—CHRISTIANITY UNPACKED

Between themselves, the Jews often referred to the Jewish people as Israel although the land was divided into various territories. The northern territory, including Nazareth, lay west of the Sea of Galilee, and was one of the territories ruled for the Romans by Herod Antipas and was called Galilee. The southern territory, including Jerusalem, was called Judea and was ruled by the Roman prefect Pontius Pilate. Between Galilee and Judea lay the territory known as Samaria, which was also ruled by Pontius Pilate.

The Jews considered the world to be divided into two types of people: Jews and Gentiles (non-Jews), so the Jews worked hard to disassociate themselves from the Gentiles, trying to separate themselves both religiously and morally. About four million Jews lived in the Roman Empire during the first century, many of whom were dispersed throughout the empire. Although these dispersed Jews practiced the same religion as those remaining in Israel, there were differences as they could not help absorbing some of the culture and beliefs of those around them. They also spoke Greek whilst the Jews of Israel usually spoke Hebrew or Aramaic. The Romans maintained strict control over the peoples of their empire but, wisely, accepted that most people could have religious freedom, political freedom, and freedom of thought. The Jewish people accepted their freedom in both their governing system and in maintaining their own traditions, yet the Roman government required that everything be ultimately subject to Roman authority. For example, Jewish citizens were under the authority of the Jewish court system, yet all sentences for the death penalty had to be referred to the Romans. Thus most Jews resented the Roman rule and were, in the main, downtrodden subjects of both the Romans and the Jewish elite.

## The Jewish Religion

In order to understand life in the first century it is vital to understand the religious beliefs of the time as religion was central to how all people lived and thought and hence influenced every aspect of life. Although the Jews lived in a time when there were many

Gods and many religions within the Greco-Roman territories and most peoples worshiped whatever God was appropriate to their concern at the time, the Jews were different, distinct. The wider world viewed the Jews as odd but tolerated them as long as they did not cause any trouble.

## The Agreement with God

The Jewish people believed in one God (monotheism) with whom they individually, and indeed the whole of the Jewish people, had a special, personal relationship. The Jewish God was invisible and could not be portrayed, whereas the people of the surrounding cultures believed in many gods (polytheism) and they had them represented by images or idols. The Jews believed that their special relationship with God was captured by the agreement (covenant) that Moses had received from God. Common Judaism was thus characterized by this agreement between God and his chosen people of Israel. For his part God would protect and love the people of Israel and they would love God (and no other god) and keep his laws (the Law). If they did not obey the Law they would be subject to God's punishment.

## The Temple

God recognized the weaknesses of people so they could gain forgiveness for any transgression by offering sacrifices at the temple in Jerusalem, but only at the temple. There could be only one temple and it was thus the most import religious building for the Jews and was where the presence of God could be felt. The temple was central to the religious and political life of the Jews; it was where they could experience the divine presence and where any damage to their relationship with God could be repaired. So many sacrifices were offered by individuals, and by the priests on behalf of the whole Jewish nation, that the temple must have seemed like a slaughterhouse and would have been covered with blood and flies. If the Jews maintained their side of the covenant, offering sacrifices as necessary, they believed that God would also maintain God's side of the covenant, continue to reside in the temple, treat the people of Israel favorably, and they would be among those saved by God at the time of judgement.

## The High Priest

The high priests were appointed by Roman prefects or the puppet Jewish leaders who, to emphasize the authority of the occupiers, kept control of the sacred vestments that the high priest would need to wear on the most holy days. Therefore the high priest would have to regularly undergo the indignity of asking for these vestments to be made available. The high priest between 6 and 15 AD was called Ananus and, until 43 AD, the high priest was always from his family (either one of his sons or his son-in-law), apart from some very short periods totaling no more than four or five years. So although the Romans were in charge of the appointments it appears that they went along with the Jews in condoning hereditary succession. It is probable that Ananus was unpopular with the general Jewish population but remained a powerful influence in temple politics and it is also probable that he had a particular dislike of prophets, as they spoke against those in authority. It should be noted that once a person was a high priest that person was always referred to as high priest even once he was no longer in office (like modern-day American presidents, who will be called Mr./Madam President for the rest of their lives, even when someone else lives in the White House). Hence it is not always obvious in ancient texts which person is being referred to when the words "high priest" are used.

## The Priests

The main task of a priest at the temple was to butcher the animals brought for sacrifice, but they may also offer prayers, readings from the scriptures and singing. Priests from rural areas would work at the temple on a rotating basis but the majority of their time would be spent teaching and leading worship at the local synagogue.

## The Synagogue

The synagogue played a central role in the life of the local community, where they would gather on the Sabbath to hear teachings on the Law. As only about 10 percent of the population was literate, the synagogue provided a place where the local community could gather on the Sabbath to hear the sacred scriptures being read. People sat on mats, stone benches, or wooden chairs with the priest facing them. The people sang without music, a speaker would read from the Torah scrolls, and prayers would be said. The priest would provide the interpretation of the readings and give moral and religious guidance. The synagogue became the center of all Jewish life, including a place for political meetings, school for Jewish children, and a courtroom.

## Pharisees

This was a group who were given a bad press in the gospels but they were essentially an admirable lot whose mission was to examine every detail of the Law and encourage all Jews to observe the Law. Some Pharisees were also priests, but most were not and they were essentially laypeople who were very keen that God's will as expressed by the Law was followed correctly. Hence they would debate within the synagogues on how to interpret the Law and thus try to ensure that it was followed correctly.

## Wisdom

One other aspect of Jewish religion that is worthy of mention is the tradition of wisdom, which was also taught in the synagogue. The wisdom texts are recognized as having been developed by men and are thus separate from the holy scriptures that were believed to have been derived from communication with God. Wisdom is essentially a commonsense guide on how to live a good life and, in keeping with common sense, it allows these guidelines to be modified intelligently to account for individual circumstances (unlike the Law, which, being decreed by God, could not be changed). Comparable texts could be found in other religions.

## Prophets and Martyrs

Outside of the formal religious structure there was a strong Jewish tradition of prophets. The prophet got his strong sense of mission from his own conviction that he had a close relationship with God and that God spoke to him during his prayers. Nowadays any large, forward-thinking organization will recognize the value of someone who can challenge the status quo and shake up the establishment, and in Jewish religious society this was the role of the prophet. They often did not have any formal training but proclaimed that their authority came directly from God. These self-proclaimed holy men thus made it their mission to stand against the tendency of the people of Israel to drift away from God and neglect their obligations. Unlike the Pharisees, who were concerned with the details of the Law, the prophets were more interested in the big picture and hence they railed against the corrupt establishment, reminding people of the basic principles of Judaism such as the duty for piety and righteousness. Prophets typically warned against events that were to occur in the near future and urge people to mend their ways and prepare themselves before it was too late. Their message was typically uncomfortable and unwelcome, particularly for those in power (e.g., high priests), who had tended to become complacent and more interested in their own well-being than extolling piety and righteousness. As prophets were not under the control of the formal religious hierarchy, they were free to speak out against the authorities and it is thus clear that they would not have been welcomed by the temple authorities.

By definition a martyr dies for a cause, although he/she probably did not intend or want to die. The Jews believed that even if the person killed was completely faithful to God, they shared in the guilt of the nation. Thus if someone was killed it was thought to be a sign that God was angry with the people of Israel so they must have been unfaithful. Although human sacrifice was banned

LIFE FOR THE JEWS AROUND THIRTY AD

in Israel, the martyrdom of the innocent was believed to persuade God to relent and turn his righteous anger away from the people of Israel and show mercy. It was thus normal for the Jews to speak of a martyr as dying for the sins of the people.

## Family

Jewish families were usually large and boys were more valued than girls. Families had no last names and therefore were identified by their father, their occupation, their political position, or where they were from. Jews ate only two meals a day, one at midday and the other at night. They ate mostly fruit and vegetables, consuming meat only on special occasions. The husband was the spiritual and legal head of the house; he was responsible for feeding, sheltering, and protecting the family. Children were instructed early to honor their parents and a Jewish family lived by very strict moral, social, and religious rules. Parents (especially fathers) had a duty in Jewish society to teach their children about God and their obligations under the Law. Hence, together with the teachings at the synagogue, the children would understand the essential badges of Judaism:

- Worship only the one true God.
- Live a life of righteousness and piety.
- Keep the Law, especially the food laws.
- Observe the Sabbath.
- Adhere to the sacrificial system of the temple.
- Circumcision for boys—traditionally at eight days old.

Twice a day, in the morning and in the evening, the family would gather to recite prayers. Parents, unmarried children, and a married son and his spouse would often all live together under one roof but it should be understood that in first-century Israel women were considered second-class citizens. The Sabbath began on Friday at sundown and ended at Saturday sundown. Sabbath was started with prayer, the lighting of the candles by the wife of the household, followed by a joyful Friday supper. Sabbath was considered to be a day of rest and worship, where everything one did was in honor of God. The major religious holiday during the Jewish year was the Passover feast, which celebrated the deliverance of the Jewish people from their slavery in Egypt, and many Jews would travel to Jerusalem in order to celebrate in the holy city.

## John the Baptist

If we are to understand Jesus we must first understand John the Baptist, whose mission lasted from approximately 25 to 29 AD. This was a time when the Jews were in a highly emotional state, for they firmly believed that they were living in the last days of the world as they knew it. They were expecting a Messiah or savior, sent from God, who would reinvigorate the Jewish religion and bring them freedom after generations of suffering. This Messiah would be a great leader and warrior who would establish for the Jews a time of glory like that under King David. The Jews, of course, were also well aware of the wider world with all the gods, beliefs, myths etc. that existed around them. It must have been a volatile mixing pot of cultures and religious expectations. It was during this time that a charismatic prophet began preaching to the people of Israel and harangued them for not following the teachings of God. This prophet became known as John the Baptist as he offered baptism in the River Jordan as an alternative to temple sacrifices.

John was looking towards the coming of God and warned about the coming fire of God's judgement, which was not a very comfortable message for his audience to hear. The core of John's message was fundamentally Jewish, being in the mainstream of Jewish religious belief, and as such he exhorted the Jews to practice piety and righteousness. Although John offered baptism as an alternative way of redemption to temple sacrifice, he still supported the place of the temple as a central pillar of Jewish religion even if he did not support the high priests (Ananus and family). John became a very popular prophet, drawing such large crowds that

## LIFE FOR THE JEWS AROUND THIRTY AD

Herod became worried that he may spark an uprising so he had John arrested and subsequently put to death.

However, even after John's imprisonment and execution there continued to be a considerable movement dedicated to his memory and extolling his teachings.

# 4

## JESUS THE PROPHET

Before we begin the analysis of the Christian faith there are two points that are important to emphasize. The first is to repeat the warning that some of you, especially committed Christians, may be upset by what is said and find it disrespectful to be talking about Jesus in the manner of just another figure from history. The study of theology can cause people to question their faith and, in extreme cases, lead to the complete loss of faith. Conversely, others find that a greater awareness of the basis of their religion and a deeper understanding of the original intention of ancient scriptures leads to a deeper appreciation.

The second point is to acknowledge that very little about Jesus and the Christian faith is universally agreed and the best that can be presented are probabilities and possibilities about much of the life and teachings of Jesus and the early church. It is very difficult to strip away two millennia's worth of Christian influence and interpretation and get back to the Jewish way of thinking and understanding. At one extreme there are those that will declare that nothing can be known about the life of Jesus, while at the other extreme are those that declare that everything written in the New Testament was inspired by the Holy Spirit and must thus be accepted as the true word of God.

## Analyzing Sources

In this chapter I will be telling the story of the life and mission of the Jew known as Jesus of Nazareth and in the chapters that follow I will consider how he became recognized by many as Jesus the Christ and how the religion of Christianity developed until it became one of the world's major religions. In presenting the story of Christianity in this straightforward chronological manner I have tried to strip away many of the overlays of myth and fantasies that have been added over the centuries. This does, however, present the reader with difficulties as much of what is read may not match what the reader is expecting or what has been previously taught. I have deliberately not interrupted the flow of the story with lots of detailed analysis of the source materials in an attempt to justify what I have written. Please try and just read what is written, accepting it as my account of what may have happened before throwing your arms up in horror because it does not conform to what you have always thought happened. In part III of this book I will present some thoughts on the nature of Jesus and on the doctrines of the Christian faith and explain the rationale that lends credibility to those thoughts.

Of course the primary source of information about Jesus is the New Testament in the Bible and, in particular, the four gospels of Matthew, Mark, Luke and John, together with Acts and the letters of Paul. Apart from the Bible there are a few other sources, such as the writings of the Jewish historian Josephus, the Dead Sea Scrolls, and other various ancient scrolls and documents.

I will consider the background and origins of the gospels in more detail in the next chapter, but for now we do need to note that although the gospels contain much biographical information about Jesus, they must be treated with care as historical accuracy was not an important consideration for the authors. Again, in the next chapter, we will see that all the books of the New Testament were written many years after the death of Jesus and hence they look back in time to talk about a person who had since become someone who was revered and worshipped.

Traditional ways of analyzing the gospels are known as literary archaeology or historical criticism. This is where the separate sections of the text are examined in detail to highlight where it seems that bits have been added to the original stories (for example, to explain or emphasize a particular point) or where the original sayings have been edited (for example, to support the authors own theological views) or where the text seems disjointed (for example, where two stories have been merged). More recently, narrative criticism has been more popular, where the whole text is looked at to understand the techniques and devices the author has used to make the story compelling and convincing. Consideration is given to such aspects as the plot, the use of various characters, the building of tensions, anticipation of events to come, and unpredictable twists. Both these approaches have enabled scholars to get into the minds of the authors and understand what they were trying to achieve and also to truly appreciate the great skill with which the gospels were constructed. Each gospel writer understood what Jesus meant in their own individual, unique way and it simply does not work to try and harmonize the gospels. We need to recognize that while there is often no reason to doubt that such and such material does go back to Jesus, there is also quite often a need to check, using defensible tests or criteria as to whether or not it does. Any such criteria are highly controversial so there is no universal acceptance of any set of criteria. However, they may include:

- Does it fit within a first century Israeli setting?
- Are there several independent references?
- Is it typical of what a Jewish prophet would do and say?

Overall we have to be both constructive and skeptical and endeavor to search for facts rather than just accept what we have been told. All we are left with are possibilities and not certainties. It should be recognized that, although much is accepted by some people, almost nothing is agreed by everyone.

Unpicking the gospels to find the true story of Jesus is always going to involve making intelligent guesses and judgements and hence it can never result in anything more than a possible reconstruction. This is known as the search for the historical Jesus and many academics have done some excellent work in this area over the past few years; there are various worthwhile books that have been written and I would recommend Theissen and Merz's book *Historical Jesus*. I must also mention the excellent course that I attended at Sarum College in Salisbury, England, entitled "Theology Quest and Questions" and led by professor David Catchpole. Professor Catchpole is a respected academic who takes great care to present a detailed and robust analysis before offering any conclusion.

The following, therefore, is a very brief interpretation and reconstruction of the life, mission, and teachings of Jesus of Nazareth and all inaccuracies, simplifications, exaggerations, errors, etc. are entirely mine and mine alone.

## Jesus: A Prophet Is Born

Jesus was born between 6 and 4 BC in the village of Nazareth, which lay in the hills twelve miles southwest of the Sea of Galilee and had a population of between two and three hundred. The land was fertile and life was patterned by the traditions, roles, and rituals passed down through the generations. His mother, Mary, was not married at the time of her pregnancy but was engaged to Joseph, a worker in wood and stone. An unmarried woman who fell pregnant would have been the subject of a certain amount of gossip and Jesus was sometimes referred to as the son of Mary, which was a derogatory term as a boy received honor from being the son of his father, not his mother. However, Mary and Joseph did marry and had several other sons and daughters so that Jesus was raised in a large family with many siblings.

Joseph and Mary seem like a traditional Jewish couple, naming their children after the Jewish patriarchs, and they would have taught them the stories from the Torah, taken them to the local synagogue and observed the religious traditions. Jesus would have learnt the Jewish Kaddish mourner's prayer, which begins:

PART II—CHRISTIANITY UNPACKED

"Magnified and sanctified be God's great name in the world which he has created according to his will. May he establish his kingdom soon, in our lifetime"[1] (note the pleas for the kingdom to be established soon).

It is likely that Joseph would have passed on to his sons the skills of an artisan and they would also have learnt basic reading and writing, certainly sufficient to be able to carry on their trade. Not much can be known about Jesus' early life but sometime in the mid to late 20s AD he joined the movement led by the prophet John the Baptist. As mentioned in the last chapter, John was expecting the coming of a new age ruled by God so he urged the Jews to prepare by returning to the basics of the Jewish faith, repenting of all their sins, and maintaining a life of righteousness and piety. Now John was fully aware that only God could forgive sins but he offered baptism in the River Jordan as a ritual alternative to sacrifices at the temple in Jerusalem. Those being baptized would be required to confess their sins and pledge to live a righteous life in order to have a realistic hope that when God judged them their sins would be forgiven.

As a disciple of John, Jesus was himself baptized and confessed his sins. Following his baptism Jesus experienced a feeling of intense ecstasy such that he became convinced that God was calling him to devote his life to service. He entered a period of anguish and personal doubt as he wrestled with his feelings about what God wanted him to do and the knowledge of the hardship and danger that would entail. It was probably during this period that his family feared for his sanity but Jesus became absolutely convinced that God had filled him with the Spirit and thus bestowed on him the power to speak and act in his name.

By definition, John the Baptist was stuck in the location of the River Jordan where he could baptize, so Jesus decided to start off on his own and become an itinerant preacher and prophet taking the message about the coming of God to the small villages in Galilee. Jesus always remembered his debt to John and held him in the highest esteem as great among the prophets of Israel.

1. "Words of the Mourner's Kaddish."

## Jesus the Prophet

### Jesus: The Key Prophecy

Throughout the New Testament there are many instances where it is clear the main thrust of the message that Jesus brings is that "the kingdom of God has come near."[2] What Jesus meant by the kingdom of God is not explicitly explained in the gospels (probably because everyone who was expected to read the gospels knew what it meant) but it is so central to the story of Jesus that we will need to do our best to understand what was meant.

The Jews saw the kingdom of God as representing a new world, a new era in the long history of the Jewish people when justice, freedom, and compassion would prevail. God uses his power to realize his goodness on earth and also works through humans by instilling a desire for goodness. So the kingdom of God would be a wonderful time brought about by the royal intervention of God on behalf of his chosen people, a new era indeed in which poverty in all forms would be banished. Since the associations of poverty include powerlessness and lack of honor, this is a truly revolutionary message. The kingdom of God is centered on Israel but extends beyond death; it breaks down the historical distribution of power and wealth. The displaced Jews would return to Israel, many Gentiles would also come to be saved by God's mercy, foreign oppression would end, and there would be peace and justice for all.

This seems to have been regarded by Jesus as something to be proclaimed as coming into being rather soon, certain to happen, and may even be in the early stages. Jesus may have expected that he would have an important role once God's kingdom was established but that was for the future and does not mean that he saw himself as the Messiah. Rather, Jesus believed that he and John the Baptist were the last in a long line of Jewish prophets and, once John had been executed, Jesus was to be the last who would actually witness the coming of God's kingdom.

Jesus modified John the Baptist's main theme regarding the coming of God. Whilst John's main thrust was to shake up the Jews

---

2. Mark 1:15.

so they would turn to God and obey God's commandments, Jesus added a compassionate overlay regarding the unbounded mercy of God. The majority of the villagers were very poor and often hungry and the only way to survive, pay their taxes, and feed their families was to borrow money, hence they also became burdened with debts that they could not pay. To them Jesus brought hope with his message that the kingdom of God was imminent. He explained what the kingdom would mean for them by using three short beatitudes that could originally have been:

1. Blessed are the poor, for theirs is the kingdom of God.
2. Blessed are the hungry, for they shall be satisfied.
3. Blessed are those that mourn, for they shall be comforted.

He taught them how to pray in the manner of a traditional Jewish prayer: "Father, hallowed be your name. Your kingdom come. Give us each day our daily bread. And forgive us our sins, for we ourselves forgive everyone indebted to us. And do not bring us to the time of trial"[3] (note the similarities with the Kaddish prayer).

It is not difficult to see how this message would have been received joyously by the poor, downtrodden peasants in his audience. It must be remembered that the coming of God's glorious kingdom also brought with it God's judgement, so Jesus would have repeated John's call for all to repent of their sins and lead a pious and righteous life. However, Jesus modified the emphasis within John's message by highlighting the good news of the kingdom as well as the need to prepare for judgement.

## Jesus: His Teaching

As his reputation grew, more and more people came to hear Jesus preach. His charismatic personality attracted dedicated followers who were so inspired by him that they abandoned their jobs and families to be with him as he processed through Israel. Although

---

3. Luke 11:2.

Jesus was a source of comfort for the poor peasants and was considered liberal in his teachings, he demanded that his disciples made great sacrifices as they prepared for the coming kingdom. When the disciples were sent out on a mission they were instructed to "carry no purse, no bag, no sandals."[4]

- No purse meant that they had no money and were poor.
- No bag meant they had no food and were hungry.
- No sandals meant that they were mourning.

That is, they were to act out the beatitudes!

As a Jew preaching to Jews, Jesus' teachings were based on the Law and the wisdom tradition, with his central aim being to explain what the kingdom would be like and what they had to do to prepare for the coming judgement.

Jesus would himself have been taught the Jewish wisdom traditions at synagogue and also possibly by John the Baptist, who taught in the style of a wisdom teacher. Wisdom thinking is international and much of it could have originated in Egypt. It is based on experience and observations of life, e.g., "no one puts new wine into old wineskins; the wine will burst the skins, and the wine is lost, and so are the skins; but one puts new wine into fresh wineskins."[5]

It is about how to live a good life:

- Living in accordance with the experience distilled over the generations.
- Living in harmony with the created order.

Remember that wisdom is not law and is flexible depending on particular circumstances and Jesus taught with authority about wisdom sayings. Jesus' take on the wisdom teachings were often very insightful, sometimes turning traditional thoughts on their heads. Whilst his teaching sometimes sounded counterintuitive,

---

4. Luke 10:4.
5. Mark 2:21–22.

such as "Love your enemies,"[6] precedents could be found in the wisdom traditions. Thus, although Jesus is indebted to the wisdom tradition, his unique take and insights were often in conflict with the teachings of the religious establishment. For Jesus this was all a matter of the imminent arrival of the kingdom of God being the dominating issue that must be taken seriously, for it was the people who listened to Jesus and responded positively to his message who would be saved.

Jesus was able to distinguish between what was important and what was not so important and this sometimes led him to interpret the Law in a manner that upset those who stuck to a literal interpretation. It should be understood that he and the Pharisees had much in common as they, like him, were dedicated to God and thus he would often debate the application of Jewish holy law with them. Whilst Jesus was also a true believer in the Jewish faith and the application of the Law, he did not agree with the rigidly strict interpretation of the Pharisees and advocated a more flexible approach that allowed for God's mercy in understanding human needs and fragility. Thus Jesus applied the flexibility allowed within the Jewish wisdom tradition to the interpretation of the Law, providing for a more intelligent way of giving guidance on how the Law should be applied in individual circumstances. The two key teachings from Jesus, however, are in line with traditional Jewish thinking although presented in a more positive manner:

- "You shall love the Lord your God with all your heart, and with all your soul, and with all your strength, and with all your mind; and your neighbor as yourself."[7]
- "Do to others as you would have them do to you."[8]

He emphasized that the supreme expression of the will of God is the provision of mercy but in order to be sure of being granted

---

6. Matt 5:44.
7. Luke 10:27.
8. Luke 6:31.

entry into the kingdom it was not enough to just to have done no harm: it was essential to have done good.

Jesus used parables in his teaching, these being the kind of stories that would be easily remembered in a society with limited literacy and could be passed on by word of mouth. They are stories that involve the listener, perhaps starting with a question: "What do you think?" They typically describe two different approaches to a situation, making the listener think about what is the correct approach and how they personally would have behaved. Finally Jesus would hammer home the lesson by summarizing with "I tell you..."

Parables can be used to teach many things and may not necessarily have any fixed meaning. As with other types of his teachings, Jesus could give an unexpected twist to a story and hence provide a unique insight. His listeners may have gone away and discussed and debated the parable, which would have further enhanced the learning experience. For instance, in the parable of the prodigal son the elder son had been a dutiful son living a faithful Jewish life in accordance with the Law. Many of the listeners would have felt sympathy for his behavior but Jesus pointed out that he had forgotten the place of mercy in God's kingdom.

Several of the parables do not mention the kingdom explicitly but they do provide insights into what is to be expected. Even though life may seem full of failure now, when the kingdom comes life will become a fantastic success for those downtrodden peasants. He explained how God's justice will work when the kingdom dawns and the poor and downtrodden will be welcome but the rich and powerful will find it harder to gain entry. Overall, the messages of the parables are to explain the kingdom and how to prepare; not by blind obedience to the Law plus strict adherence to the rules of Jewish worship, but by love and mercy and true repentance. Piety and righteousness are repeated themes.

PART II—CHRISTIANITY UNPACKED

## Jesus: The Working of Wonders

There were many people in the ancient world that were regarded as wonder workers so when Jesus performed such feats he was doing, in many ways, nothing that was unique or exceptional. Within the culture of the time it would have been accepted by those present as part of the way things were. The working of wonders, particularly the driving out of demons, was used by Jesus to reinforce his prophecy of the coming of the kingdom of God by declaring that such acts were signs of the nearness of the kingdom.

Although diseases and disabilities were regarded at the time as being caused by demons or a punishment by God, the cure of such physical ailments needs to be considered separately from the cure of mental illnesses and emotional problems. The wonders worked by Jesus are thus divided into three categories:

- exorcisms.
- healings.
- nature miracles.

### *Exorcisms*

Jesus would have absolutely believed that he was filled with the spirit and had God's authority over the demons that possessed the unfortunate. This self-belief, combined with immense charisma, would have easily convinced the afflicted and those around them that here was someone who had authority over the demons. Everybody would have accepted that possession by demons was the cause of disturbed behavior and that a holy man like Jesus could drive out those demons and hence resolve the problems.

### *Healings*

It was understood that it was God, and God alone, who could heal so therefore prayer was the normal way to obtain healing. Doctors were not generally respected as they were expensive, not very effective, and only considered at best to be helping God in his healing. Faith healers were by far more popular (and cheaper) and they were generally considered to be more effective than doctors. In accordance with the belief that it was God who was the ultimate healer the faith healer would normally offer up prayers for the sick to be healed. Jesus was different in that he had the authority of a prophet to personally declare that the person had been healed by God. However, any healing required the absolute faith of the sick person, or the faith of those around them, that this charismatic prophet truly had that authority. Being cured was thus seen as being saved by faith and it is likely that people began to magnify his healing abilities and attribute amazing feats to him.

## *Nature Miracles*

The New Testament includes several nature miracles by Jesus such as calming a storm or walking on water. In the Old Testament it is only God who performs miracles so that the ability to perform miracles such as walking on water became a standard test for those who claimed divinity. I shall leave further consideration of Jesus and the nature miracles to part III, where I share some thoughts regarding such supernatural feats and why the gospel writers included them in the gospels.

## Jesus: The Temple

For the Jews the temple in Jerusalem was a special place where God's presence could be encountered and it would be expected that Jesus also would have gone there several times during his life to celebrate the major religious festivals. Although the Jews believed God resided in the temple, this does not mean that they thought that he was somehow contained within the temple, as he could be worshiped or found anywhere. Indeed, if God was displeased with the Jews he could remove his presence from the temple, which would also mean that his protection for the temple was gone.

Although Jesus was a believer in the special significance of the temple, this does not mean that he supported the temple authorities who were associated with social injustice and oppression—a "den of robbers."[9] There were precedents for Jewish prophets to go to the temple, attract attention by creating a disturbance, and then to preach and prophesize, and it was almost inevitable that Jesus would do likewise.

He arranged to travel to Jerusalem just before the feast of Passover, when the city would be full of pilgrims visiting the temple. Jesus organized for himself an entry into Jerusalem that proclaimed that he believed that in the kingdom of God, which he expected to dawn very soon, he would have a key role to play and be like royalty was on earth. He thus arrived with his group of disciples and followers and as he rode a colt into the city they made a loud proclamation that he was blessed, laying cloaks and leafy branches in his path. This must have both startled the local residents and concerned the authorities, who were already nervous of retaining control during the highly charged atmosphere of the festival. Jerusalem was in Judea one of the Roman provinces ruled by a prefect called Pontius Pilate, although the Jewish high priest, Caiaphas (son in law of Ananus), was in charge on a day-to-day basis but remained answerable to the Romans if anything went wrong.

A couple of days before Passover Jesus went to the temple determined to get noticed and make all aware that they must prepare for the imminent arrival of God's kingdom. The temple was an extremely large collection of interconnected buildings. Jews had travelled long distances to worship at the temple and to offer their sacrifices in accordance with their agreement with God but it was impractical to bring the sacrificial animals with them. It was thus necessary for the temple authorities to ensure that there were suitable arrangements for the pilgrims to exchange their money and buy the sacrificial animals. However, in order to gain attention, Jesus deliberately interrupted the smooth operation of the business of the temple by shouting, upturning tables, and physically stopping worshippers as they walked past. Soon a large crowd had gathered to see what all the noise was about so Jesus began to preach and, as a prophet, declare that he was speaking in the name

9. Matt 21:13.

of the God of Israel and had every right to do so within the house of God. He spoke against the temple authorities, warning that God would leave the temple because of their behavior. He spoke about the coming kingdom of God and how this temple that humans had built would be destroyed by God and replaced by a marvelous temple that God would build. Overall this was not only a provocative act but a revolutionary message that would strike at the heart of both the Jewish and Roman authorities.

*Jesus was a typical Jewish prophet preaching to the common Jews. His mission was to explain to them how to prepare for the imminent arrival of the kingdom of God and what to expect.*

## Jesus: The Trial and Execution

The Jews believed that God would test the faithfulness of his people and they would often pray that they may be spared this time of trial or temptation. Jesus himself must have believed that he, as God's prophet, would be a prime candidate to undergo God's test of his faithfulness, although he too prayed that he would be spared. Jesus knew full well that what he had done at the temple was not only provocative but potentially personally dangerous especially in light of the recent beheading of John the Baptist. However, he was totally convinced that he spoke for God and thus he was dedicated to his mission of declaring the dawning of the kingdom of God.

On the day before the Passover festival he hosted a meal for twelve of his most dedicated followers, when the atmosphere would have been dominated by the thoughts of Israel's identity and history. While they were eating Jesus took some bread and broke and gave it to his disciples saying, "This is my body."[10] The bread would have been understood by the Jewish disciples as symbolic of the person of Jesus and by sharing it they reinforced their bond with him. Later in that day they had supper and afterwards Jesus took a cup of wine drank from it and passed it around saying, "This

---

10. Luke 22:19.

cup that is poured out for you is the new covenant in my blood."[11] Again the disciples would have understood that they were all committing themselves to his vision of a new era in God's kingdom where God's laws would be kept by all (unlike the then-present time when the covenant with God was repeatedly being broken by the unfaithfulness of the people).

As he had anticipated, the authorities of the high priest were nervous that Jesus was a threat to public order and they decided that they had to act before things got completely out of hand, hence they had Jesus arrested. We can only imagine what went through his mind when he was arrested:

- Was this God's test of his faithfulness?
- His time of trial?
- Would the kingdom of God dawn and save him?

The Roman prefect Pontius Pilate was in Jerusalem and he was always wary of the troublesome Jews and their religion; he knew passions ran high during Passover. The high priest questioned Jesus before sending him to Pontius Pilate with a recommendation that he be sentenced to death. The official charge that resulted in Jesus being crucified was that he had claimed to be "the King of the Jews"[12] and this title was nailed to the cross. When Jesus was questioned by both the Jewish high priest and again by the Roman prefect he did not deny the charge. It was the practice that when members of the lower classes rebelled against the state the barbaric method of execution by crucifixion was used as a way of deterring others. Crucifixion was an awful way to die.

For the disciples of Jesus his execution was devastating:

- All their certainties had been demolished and they did not know what to do.
- God's kingdom was to have been a reality in the lifetime of Jesus.

11. Luke 22:20.
12. Matt 27:37.

- Jesus had been so filled with God's presence, so charismatic, and so authoritative that they had given up everything to dedicate themselves to him and to God.
- Now it seemed that Jesus had been wrong and that they had been abandoned.
- They ran away or denied that they had known him despite having dedicated themselves to him at the meal just a short time ago.
- They were not only extremely frightened but also ashamed of themselves.

In the next chapter I examine how the Jewish prophet known as Jesus of Nazareth came to be considered as the promised Jewish Messiah—the Christ.

# 5

## JESUS DECLARED AS THE CHRIST

Many people refer to Jesus Christ as if Christ is a surname or family name, whereas it is actually a title meaning the anointed one, the one sent by God to save the Jewish people as prophesied in the Old Testament. I shall hence use the phrase Jesus the Christ rather than just Jesus Christ. The word Christ comes from the ancient Greek for the anointed one, whilst the Hebrew/Aramaic equivalent word is Messiah. So how did the ancient Jewish prophet Jesus of Nazareth come to be worshiped as the Christ/Messiah?

### Resurrection?

"He has been raised."[1] For those distraught and traumatized disciples the impact of the resurrection must have been completely overwhelming. The Christian religion cannot exist without belief in the resurrection of Jesus of Nazareth and, because it is of such fundamental importance, I shall return more than once to discuss it further in part III, where I will attempt to gain some insight into what may have actually happened. For those of you who wish

---

1. Matt 28:6.

to delve deeper into the resurrection I would recommend Allison's *Resurrecting Jesus*. The resurrection of the prophet Jesus of Nazareth was to become the key event that defined the Christian religion, but what did the Jews mean when they said he was resurrected? Was it that the body of Jesus that was supposedly wrapped and placed in a tomb had miraculously recovered and he was alive again? Was it that Jesus was no longer made of flesh and blood but had become a spiritual being with a transformed heavenly body? Unfortunately the New Testament stories are inconsistent so yet again I have to turn to the work of the scholars to search for the most probable explanation.

It is most likely that those who testified that they had seen the risen Jesus had had some sort of personal experience that convinced them that Jesus had somehow survived death and had become a heavenly being. These experiences ranged from visual appearances, to hearing his voice, to just having an overwhelming feeling that he was present with them. These experiences may have happened while asleep or whilst awake but they had such a significant impact on those that had them that they were convinced that the experiences were real. In this chapter I will consider the hundred years following the crucifixion of Jesus and it is important to understand how the events unfolded in a chronological order. Although it is not possible to provide precise dates for all the events, I have attempted to provide dates that are a reasonable approximation based on what the majority of scholars calculate. These can be found in the time line presented at the end of this chapter. I must emphasize that these dates should not be taken as absolute (e.g., some estimate the year of the crucifixion as 30 AD whilst others as 33 AD) but their purpose is to help grasp the overall timeline and the sequence of events.

## The Jesus Movement

After Jesus was killed his followers were distraught; they did not know what to do. All their certainties that the kingdom of God would soon become a reality and they would have a significant role alongside Jesus had been demolished. Now Jesus had been killed, his mission ended, and they had been abandoned. However, the disciples, like all the Jews, still believed that they were living in the last days before the kingdom of God would be established and all the dead would be resurrected.

A few days after his crucifixion, Mary Magdalene was the first person to have an experience of a risen Jesus. After Mary several other people reported similar experiences and Jesus was also reported as having appeared to groups of people. Importantly one of his principle disciples, called Peter, and one of the brothers of Jesus, James, had these experiences and they thus began to believe that Jesus had somehow survived death to be resurrected by God in some transformed, heavenly manner. They had renewed hope that what Jesus had told them was indeed true and that the kingdom of God was indeed near.

They went into the synagogues in Jerusalem and the surrounding areas to talk about Jesus and his teachings and how he had been resurrected. This became known as the Jesus movement within the Jewish faith and its influence began to spread. As the disciples talked about Jesus they were remembering what he said and did. Undoubtedly, like all of us tend to do when we talk about the recently departed, they exaggerated his good points, talking about him as a great and wise teacher who performed wondrous deeds. Thus they began the process of idolizing their dead master, whom they believed had been saved from death by God. However, there was opposition within some synagogues about what the teachings of Jesus meant, especially his more liberal interpretations of the Law. Jesus' mission as a prophet was to shake up the Jews and bring them back to the basics of their religion so that the agreement with God was kept and God could establish his kingdom. Those in the Jesus movement thus still considered themselves to be part of the Jewish faith, worshiping the same God and following the Jewish religious law, keeping to the food laws, attending the synagogue and the temple, and practicing circumcision of boys.

This Jesus movement was tolerated by the synagogues as long as they did nothing to affront the central Jewish belief in the one

## Jesus Declared as the Christ

God; however, these followers of Jesus soon began to say that he was lord and should also be worshiped. This was too much for the Jews and they were thus expelled from the synagogues and had to worship as a separate sect although they still thought of themselves as Jews following the Law and the other badges of Judaism. However, they associated Jesus with the expected Jewish Messiah, the promised savior of the Jewish people who would be sent by God. They knew he had been human during his life and at his death but believed he had been transformed at his resurrection to be seen as the Messiah. Hence the cult became known as the Christians—the Greek translation of Messiah.

## A Jew from Tarsus

The Jew from Tarsus known as Paul (originally Saul) was born about the same time as Jesus (although they never met); he was a tent maker by trade and appears to have been very clever and dynamic but physically small and not in possession of much charisma. He was a Pharisee who took a passionate dislike to the teachings of the Jesus movement. We do not have access to any independent information about the pre-Christian Paul as we mainly know of him in the New Testament via his letters and the book of Acts (written by the author of the gospel attributed to Luke). About three years after the death of Jesus, Paul was in Damascus when he also had a vision of Jesus. This was an intense and personal experience and must have made a huge impact on Paul as it caused him to completely change what he was doing with his life and he dedicated the remainder of his days to spreading his message about Jesus. It is possible that Paul had further Jesus experiences as it is written that on several occasions he fell into a trance. Indeed, it has even been postulated that he was an epileptic but this is probably not so. However, following his experiences of Jesus Paul was convinced that he had a mission from God to tell people that Jesus had been resurrected; he was alive and would return. I shall discuss further in part III some possible explanations for

PART II—CHRISTIANITY UNPACKED

Paul's experiences, although it has to be acknowledged that after two thousand years it is impossible to be certain.

Although many regard Paul as the most significant theologian of his time and the chief architect of the Christian faith, it is not easy to gain a clear understanding of Paul's beliefs regarding how God worked through Jesus. This may be because Paul himself seemed to sometimes struggle with conflicting concepts and developed his own understanding over many years. At the start of his mission, and for several years, Paul continued preaching a Christian version of Judaism, like that of the Jesus movement in Jerusalem, still based on the Law. He travelled throughout Arabia for three years before going to Jerusalem to visit Peter and James, the brother of Jesus. He stayed with Peter for fifteen days and would have had an opportunity to learn about the life and teachings of Jesus from one of those closest to him. However, to Paul the important fact about Jesus was that he had been resurrected and what he did and said during his life on earth was only of secondary importance. Paul was convinced that Jesus had been sent by God to save the people of the world, who were all living under the influence of Sin (with a capital S to signify the personification of sin). The Jesus movement understood Jesus' death to be sacrificial, atoning for the fact that Israel had not kept faithfully to their side of the agreement (i.e., like a martyr). Paul further developed this concept so that all who truly accept Jesus as their savior become one with him and would have a share in his death and resurrection and are thus released from the controlling influence of Sin. By having faith in Jesus a person would belong to a group who would be saved from Sin and they would begin to be transformed to a new existence that would be completed with the return of Jesus.

The Jesus movement based in Jerusalem was still heavily influenced by its Jewish roots and required all Gentile converts to become Jews, however, Paul began to take a radically different path and preached that faith in Jesus was the only requirement for salvation. Hence for Paul it was not necessary to become Jewish with all that entailed, especially male circumcision and keeping the Law

## Jesus Declared as the Christ

and the Sabbath. Paul therefore held that non-Jews (the Gentiles) were welcome to join the family of Jesus the Christ.

Paul's message to the Gentiles can be summarized as follows:

1. There is only one God (and, by the way, you should stop worshipping idols).
2. God will come and judge.
3. Salvation is available to anyone who has faith in Jesus, who has been raised from the dead by God.

Paul preached, "There is no longer Jew or Greek [Gentile], there is no longer slave or free, there is no longer male and female; for all of you are one in Christ Jesus."[2]

The promise of salvation by means of baptism and faith in Jesus must have had great appeal to many who heard Paul speak. Although these converts were not required to become Jews and obey the Law, Paul urged that they should live to the highest of moral and ethical standards but it is clear from Paul's letters that his followers often fell far short of these standards.

Paul travelled widely, preaching to the Gentiles, but after fourteen years he returned to Jerusalem to iron out some differences with the leaders of the Jesus movement. They agreed that Paul could continue with his mission to the Gentiles while Peter would lead the mission to the Jews. This agreement held for some time but the leaders in Jerusalem still had significant misgivings about the extent to which Paul allowed obedience to the Jewish law to be disregarded. It should be noted that to become a follower of Jesus was a big personal commitment for many people, not only with respect to keeping the faith in Jesus but also because it meant that you became different to the rest of your community and lost friends and family. It was thus vital for mutual support that believers in Jesus formed new friendships and became part of the family of Jesus the Christ, where the sharing of meals was an essential part of forming and reinforcing these new bonds. In many of the new churches there were converts who were Jews and

2. Gal 3:28.

converts who were Gentiles but when a Gentile hosted a meal the food served may not conform to the Jewish food laws and it was this that finally broke the agreement between Paul and the church in Jerusalem. The leaders of the church in Jerusalem included a brother of Jesus and others who were disciples of Jesus who had personally known him and heard him preach, so they claimed they had a greater authority than Paul for defining Christianity. They disowned the preaching of Paul and began to actively harass his mission. Thus the Christian churches began to split.

Paul began to write the letters that today form part of the New Testament. Jesus had been convinced that the kingdom of God would soon become a reality and Paul in his turn was convinced that Jesus would soon return to earth and that God was urging him to convert the Gentiles before Jesus returned so they could be saved and be transformed. Paul thus continued fighting for his own interpretation of the message of salvation by faith in Jesus until he was imprisoned in about 60 AD.

The key aspect for Paul was that belief in Jesus triggered a fundamental change in people so that Jesus was alive in them and they thus become part of those who would be saved whilst the non-believers would be destroyed. Remembering that Paul had once been a Pharisee implies that he must have faced many personal issues in trying to align his previous passionate Judaism with his new understanding that God had acted to free the entire world from bondage to Sin through the life, death, and resurrection of Jesus the Christ. When he preached to the Jews, who had also been brought up to believe that they were the chosen people who had a special agreement with God, he had to address why there was a change in their agreement with God. He explained to the Jews that the resurrection of Jesus heralded a new age that replaced the old age of the agreement with God, which had included the need to observe the Law. It has to be understood that Paul was preaching a fundamentally new and radically different way for the Jews to understand both the concept of messiahship and the concept of the people of God. This was a very challenging message for the Jews to accept.

For Paul there was no longer a need to comply with the badges of Judaism because salvation through faith in Jesus was available to all, both Gentiles and Jews. Paul believed that we are all able to achieve salvation by having faith in Jesus as the son of God and by this faith we are continuously being changed from within to become more in the image of God. Paul fully expected that Jesus as lord would soon return to earth and reign as the whole of creation would be transformed into a new creation that would last for eternity without any decay. The bodies of those who had faith in Jesus, whether dead or alive, would complete their changes to become transformed spiritual bodies such as Paul believed he had experienced in the risen Christ.

*Paul had radically reinterpreted the significance of Jesus from a prophet who preached about the kingdom of God to a promise of salvation to those who believed in the resurrection.*

Paul believed that his mission was to bring belief in the God of Israel to the Gentiles but his teachings regarding how faith in Jesus superseded the previous traditions of Judaism led to continued harassment from the leaders of the Jesus movement in Jerusalem.

We have already noted that Jews were spread throughout the Roman Empire and that they had been given special dispensation to allow them to continue with their religious practices. This dispensation, though, did not apply to the Christians, who had been expelled from the synagogues. By their refusal to worship the gods of the Roman Empire and to take part in sacrifices to these gods the Christians generated much hostility, so that when in 64 AD a great fire broke out in Rome the emperor Nero found it very convenient to blame these unpopular Christians. Many Christians were rounded up and put to death, although pardons were offered to those who renounced their religion and offered sacrifices to the Roman gods. Paul, Peter, and James were all killed during this period, probably in Rome.

Meanwhile in Israel the great Jewish revolt against the Roman occupation began in 66 AD but this did not go well for the Jews. In 70 AD the Romans sacked Jerusalem, destroying the temple, and by 74 AD the revolt had been well and truly quashed in the most brutal of ways. It is hard to imagine how devastating it must have been for the Jews to have their temple destroyed. Here resided the divine presence and it was where sacrifices could be made to keep the relationship with that divine being in good order. God would not have allowed the temple to be destroyed whilst he was in residence so the only possible explanation was that God was angry with Israel due to the disobedience of the Jews and had left the temple, which also removed his protection. Where was God going to reside now? It was not just a catastrophe for the Jews but also for those Christians who still followed the Jewish laws and worshiped at the temple.

## The Written Word

The New Testament is the source of most of our information regarding Jesus and is the basis of much of the Christian faith. For many people it represents the word of God as they believe that the men who wrote it were themselves inspired by God's Holy Spirit. The early Jesus movement had had no such need for written material about Jesus because many had been with him and heard him preach that God's kingdom would come very soon. They were convinced that Jesus had been resurrected by God and that he was the promised Messiah and hence their main focus was to prepare themselves for his second coming and the kingdom of God. Paul wrote letters to inspire, teach, and occasionally rebuke the members of churches scattered throughout the ancient world but he too was expecting the second coming. However, time was passing and without the second coming there would inevitably come a time when there was nobody left who had any firsthand knowledge of Jesus. The established oral traditions of the region meant that the teachings of Jesus and the stories about him would be passed on to the next generation but there would eventually be a need for these to be written down. Remember that only a small percentage of the population could read, so any written material would have to be read aloud in the churches for the new generation of Christian preachers to interpret and hence pass on the message about Jesus.

In order to grasp how the writings in the New Testament relate to each other and how one author may have built on the writing of earlier works, it is necessary to refer to the approximate timeline of events presented at the end of this chapter.

## The Letters of Paul

Paul's letters are the earliest documents written about Jesus that we have in the New Testament and as such they should be accorded the appropriate significance and respect. After his death (in about 63 AD) someone collected together several of the letters that were attributed to Paul. Paul's first letter was 1 Thessalonians, written in about 50 AD, and all his letters were probably written within a period of less than ten years. That is between twenty and thirty years after the death of Jesus. There are seven letters attributed to Paul whose genuineness is never seriously questioned: Romans, 1 Corinthians, 2 Corinthians, Galatians, Philippians, 1 Thessalonians, and Philemon. The other letters in the New Testament may have been written by some of his followers, perhaps after his death.

## A Collection of Sayings and Stories

There is evidence of an earlier work (which is known by the letter Q) being compiled in the 40s or 50s AD mainly comprised of the sayings of Jesus but also some stories. This work has been lost and no copies exist but many believe that extracts of it can be seen in some of the gospels. It has to be noted that although many scholars accept this concept and the existence of Q, there are also some respected scholars who do not.

## The Gospels

The gospels are examples of ancient biographical writings but we must be very clear that they are definitely not to be confused with modern biographies. Historical accuracy in ancient times was not seen to be as important as ensuring that the message received by the reader was consistent with the message that the author was sending. Thus if the author believed in Jesus as the Messiah and wanted to ensure that the reader was also convinced that Jesus was the promised Messiah, then that was a far more important truth to convey than any other fact.

Ancient biographies typically tell the story of a hero figure who dominates the story. The gospel authors thus tell the story of Jesus in a manner that would be appropriate at the time of writing and for the people that would receive it. All the authors of the gospels were already convinced that Jesus had been resurrected by God and that he was the promised Messiah, as can be seen in the very first sentence of Mark's gospel: "The beginning of the good news of Jesus Christ, the Son of God."[3] To ensure that the listener would also be convinced they had a large amount of Jewish religious scriptures that they could adapt to show that Jesus did indeed fulfill God's plan and meet all the expectations and requirements of the Messiah as set out in the Jewish scriptures.

The authors would feel free to modify and adjust the story to support their own beliefs and theological stance. They believed Jesus had been resurrected and transformed into a heavenly being possessing all the associated powers and capabilities. In keeping with the traditions of ancient biographies they felt free to reflect back in time so that Jesus also possessed heavenly abilities during his earthly life, such as the ability to walk on water.

Although the four gospels present different pictures of Jesus, they were all written for groups of believers who already accepted the resurrection faith. They were meant to reinforce that faith and to inspire the recipients in the worship of the risen lord rather than simply, or even primarily, to give a factual account of Jesus' life. They were not the sort of records a neutral historian would have written.

*The gospels were written many years after the death of Jesus of Nazareth to convince the reader that he was the promised Jewish*

---

3. Mark 1:1.

## Jesus Declared as the Christ

*Messiah who had been resurrected to life by God. They are not historically accurate accounts.*

By the time the gospels were written the Christian communities had many difficulties to face:

- Hostility by both the Romans and the Jews.
- Being barred from the synagogues.
- The destruction of the temple.
- Understanding why God had not yet established his kingdom as Jesus had prophesied.
- Determining how to treat the Gentiles, especially those who wished to join in Christian worship.
- Deciding whether to follow the Christianity of the Jesus movement in Jerusalem or that of Paul.

All the gospel authors therefore had to adapt their stories to address these difficulties that their readers faced in the world outside their Christian community as well as promoting their understanding of the faith. They compiled the gospels with great skill and they are remarkably accomplished pieces of writing.

Today we cannot be certain who the intended recipients of the gospels were or who were the authors (the naming of the authors occurred much later). All the gospels show signs of being edited and changed after they were originally written and John's gospel in particular looks like two separate versions have been "cut and pasted" to create the version we now read. The gospels present differing perspectives on a core of events. Those events had already been interpreted twice; first by the oral retelling, and then by the gospel writers. So what we have is not how things actually happened but how different people interpreted the disclosures of God that came to them or their teachers, through the events of Jesus' life. There is no concern for consistency, dispassionate recounting, or strict historical accuracy.

Of the four gospels in the Bible it was originally thought that Matthew came first, then Mark, Luke, and John (hence the order in the Bible), but nowadays it is generally accepted that Mark was the first to be written, in about 70 AD, i.e., forty years after the death of Jesus. When Matthew and Luke wrote their gospels over ten years after Mark many scholars believe they adapted sections from both Q and Mark to add to their own content. These first three gospels in the Bible have a common structure and tell a similar story and are hence known as the synoptic (or similar) gospels. The synoptic gospels see Jesus as the promised king of Israel bringing the kingdom of God near but although they are similar, the version of Christianity they are presenting is not the same. The fourth gospel, by John, was the last to be written and presents an entirely different Jesus.

## The Gospel According to Mark

Mark creates a general sense of urgency especially during the first phase of Jesus' mission and presents Jesus as a figure of power who engenders conflict. There is an underlying theme of misunderstanding by the disciples over who Jesus is whilst we, the readers, do know because Mark tells us at the start. The great mystery of this gospel is its sudden ending; was this intentional or was it never finished? Perhaps the ending has been lost. It is the shortest of the gospels and has no infancy stories, no temptation narrative, and no resurrection sightings.

Overall Mark appears to be a supporter of Paul's version of Christianity, presenting Jesus as a supremely powerful authoritative yet a strangely secret messianic king. Jesus' mission was undertaken entirely within Israel and he therefore had no need to give any guidance on how to relate to Gentiles but Mark, as an advocate of a liberal, inclusive Christianity, found it necessary to portray Jesus as doing away with some of the Jewish law.

## The Gospel According to Matthew

Matthew was possibly a tax collector from Capernaum on the border between Judea and Syria. Matthew is much more inclined towards the Peter/James version of Christianity and presents Jesus as a new, more powerful Moses, teaching the Torah and absolute adherence to the divine law. Thus for Matthew any Gentile who wished to become a Christian should first become a Jew and conform to the Law. For Matthew Christians were an exclusive community compared to the inclusive vision of Christianity promoted by Mark and Paul.

Despite the above, in a very bold and controversial move, Matthew includes stories where people worship Jesus even though Jews maintain there is only one God and only he may be worshipped. The Christian community for which Matthew was writing had already been banished from the synagogues as they were regarded as heretics so they evolved into a Jewish sect adhering to the Jewish religious practices with greater rigor than the Jews themselves

## The Gospel According to Luke

Unlike the other gospels, Luke wrote a two-volume story about Jesus: the gospel and Acts, but although written together they have been separated in the Bible. Most scholars date Luke to the early 80s AD, i.e., after the destruction of the temple, when the Jews had to rethink some of their religion so that it could continue without the vital aspect of temple sacrifices. It is also possible the Luke did not have access to the letters of Paul given the discrepancies between the letters and Acts (e.g., Acts 15 and Galatians).

Luke's focus is on freedom and he writes a poetic account of Jesus as the savior who reaches out to the poor and the Gentiles. Freedom is seen as:

- The forgiveness of sins.
- Liberation from the power of the devil.
- Release from oppression.

There are many parables in Luke; some of them, like the Good Samaritan and the Prodigal Son, occur only in Luke. This approach by Luke is in keeping with the traditional ways of teaching by the Jews where stories are told to illustrate the messages of the scriptures. In many of the stories Jesus is shown to turn the tables on his listeners from the expected outcome or learning. A core teaching in Luke is about the need for the rich to be charitable and to feed the poor if they are to be found worthy of heaven. Luke's gospel is also notable for the number of women included in the stories and, in particular, it describes how rich women were the patrons for the mission of Jesus. Interestingly the gospels agree that all the witnesses of the empty tomb were women, which is particularly noteworthy because the testimony of women was considered to be inferior to that of men.

Luke seems to generally support the version of Christianity promoted by Paul, although the expected imminent return of Jesus following the crucifixion seems to have faded and the church is there for the long term, which is different from Paul, who still expected the early return of Jesus.

## The Gospel According to John

The final gospel, by John, sometimes called the fourth gospel, was written around seventy years after the death of Jesus and is quite distinctive from the other three gospels regarding the picture of Jesus presented. John's gospel begins with a great poetic prologue that has inspired generations of Christians. The eternal word of God, existing before all time; Jesus as a mystical figure who was with God prior to his time on earth and who returned to God after his crucifixion. The gospel was probably written for a community in Asia Minor, which was an area heavily influenced by Greek culture and traditions. John's gospel also appears to have been heavily influenced by Greek philosophical ideas such as the eternal word and it portrays a very cosmic view of Jesus that would have been familiar to the Greek-influenced community. The main message from Jesus in the synoptic gospels is centered on the coming of the kingdom of God but John's gospel is all about a Jesus who reveals that he is indeed the one who has come to reveal. He speaks openly about being the son of God and calls people to have belief in him.

The teaching of the kingdom of God, being largely spiritualized, no longer deals with straightforward historical and political events.

The crucifixion and subsequent resurrection are presented as the final victory, with an uncompromising call to faith providing little flexibility for human weakness.

## The End of the Jesus Movement

In about 132 AD the Jews rose up again in revolt against their oppressors. This time they were led by a charismatic warrior called Simon Bar Kokhba, who finally drove the Romans out of Jerusalem, gaining control for the next three years. For many Jews, Simon Bar Kokhba seemed to be the mighty warrior and leader that God had promised and they proclaimed him as the Messiah. However, yet again the Romans returned to smash the rebellion and drive all the Jews out of Jerusalem. This was also the end of the Jesus movement in Jerusalem and the Jewish people are still waiting for their Messiah.

By the end of this period Christianity was already developing the disagreements and divisions that have become a major characteristic of nearly all organized religions. It seems that the key message of Jesus about the imminent arrival of the kingdom of God was becoming far less of an issue than belief in the resurrection. You may find it interesting to consider which Jew is actually the founder of Christianity—the one from Nazareth or the one from Tarsus. (I shall wait until part III before I present various thoughts regarding the founding of the Christian faith that may help answer that question.)

In the next chapter we look at how Christianity grew to become a huge, powerful, and bureaucratic church.

PART II—CHRISTIANITY UNPACKED

## An Approximate Timeline

| 20s and 30s AD | - Mission of John: late 20s AD<br>- Mission of Jesus of Nazareth: early 30s AD<br>- Crucifixion of Jesus: 33 AD |
|---|---|
| Mid-30s to 60 AD | - Conversion of Paul: about 36 AD<br>- Q compiled: 40–50 AD<br>- Paul's letters: written 50–60 AD |
| 60s and 70s AD | - Death of Paul: about 63 AD<br>- Jewish revolt: 66 AD<br>- Temple destroyed: 70 AD; Gospel of Mark |
| 80s and 90s AD | - Gospels of Matthew and Luke: 80–90 AD |
| 100 AD | - Gospel of John: about 100 AD |
| 130s AD | - Second Jewish revolt: 132 AD<br>- Jews driven from Jerusalem<br>- End of Jesus movement |

# 6

## THE QUEST TO UNDERSTAND

In the previous chapter I considered the original reasons why the texts that were to become the New Testament were written but it should be recognized that they expressed beliefs that were still in the course of development and that they do not provide a consistent and comprehensive blueprint for a faith. Thus during the last two thousand years humankind has been on a quest to make sense of the life, death, and resurrection of the Jewish prophet known as Jesus of Nazareth, who became hailed as Jesus the Christ. It should be noted that in chapter 4 I was mainly writing about the mission of Jesus that lasted approximately three years, whilst in chapter 5 I covered the following one hundred years. In order to bring the story of Christianity up to date I now have to condense nearly two thousand years of theological debates and arguments into this chapter. Once again I would wish to emphasize that the aim of this book is to present the big picture and not to dwell on the details. I will briefly consider various historical periods and explore the stories that shaped Christianity and how the Christian faith we have today came into being. The aim is to provide a flavor of how humankind has developed our ideas and concept of the Christian faith and how those ideas have evolved and changed over the centuries. In this chapter I will not dwell on the credibility of any aspect of this changing faith but leave those considerations until part III. It is not intended to be read as a history of Christianity but if you are interested there are literally thousands of books written about all aspects of Christianity and many of them are worth reading. Three books that I found particularly helpful are McGrath's *Heresy: A History of Defending the Truth* and *Theology: The Basics*, and Whittock and Whittock's *Christ: The First 2000 Years*.

## The Early Years

All those who had actually known Jesus were in favor of keeping the Law and following the Jewish scriptures just as Jesus had done and taught. It seems very likely, therefore, that the members of the Jesus movement in Jerusalem continued with these practices even after the deaths of the founders. However, as mentioned in the previous chapter, the Jewish uprising in 132 AD led to the Jews being driven out of Jerusalem and the extinction of the Jesus movement, thus leaving the followers of Paul, scattered throughout the empire, as the sole inheritors and advocates of Christianity. The Jews themselves eventually came to distance themselves from Jesus, rejecting him as the promised Messiah, and in the collection of ancient Jewish texts known as the Talmud it declares that he had "practiced magic (exorcisms) and led Israel astray."

In the first half of the second century AD some agreement began to emerge within the Christian communities on the group of texts that would eventually become the New Testament. As time passed Jesus' call to wait for the coming of the kingdom of God had to be rethought and it became reinterpreted as the call to be united in God, trusting in the Holy Spirit to slowly transform human lives into divine likeness. This was a huge departure from the original messages of the New Testament (e.g., Matthew's messianic Judaism, John's theology of the incarnate Logos (word of God), Paul's expectations for the early return of the Lord).

For many years after the death of Jesus, the various Christian congregations developed many different ways of understanding his nature and significance. Some thought he was a traditional Jewish prophet trying to re-energize the Jewish faith whilst others thought he sought a departure from the traditional Jewish practices and faith. Many texts within the New Testament indicate that Jesus was indeed a human being who sometimes felt tired, thirsty, and hungry whilst other texts suggested he was more than human and in some sense divine. The idea of someone being both a God and a human seemed completely illogical and incoherent so some thought he was completely human whilst others thought he was totally divine. Since it was firmly believed that it was through your faith in Jesus the Christ that you would be saved it was vital to understand how humanity and divinity were combined in Christ, for if you did not have a correct understanding of the nature of Christ you may risk your salvation. Three different approaches to this dilemma illustrate the wide diversity of opinions:

1. There were those that maintained that Jesus was human but had been filled with the Holy Spirit in the same way as the earlier prophets but more so. This is known as Adoptionism.
2. On the other hand, there were those who argued that Jesus was completely divine, but appeared to be human and thus shared in our weaknesses. This is known as Docetism.
3. The third approach is attributed to Arius, who lived in what is now Egypt at the beginning of the fourth century. He argued that Jesus was human and not divine but had been blessed by God with an understanding of God so that he could make known to humanity God's nature and God's will. But note that this understanding was provided by God to Jesus, whom God had created. Jesus the Christ was not God. This is known as Arianism and has risen in popularity many times over the past two thousand years but each time it has been put down by the church.

PART II — CHRISTIANITY UNPACKED

## Of Emperors and Creeds

Distrust of Christianity within the Roman Empire led to harassment and sporadic periods of persecution until, in 311 AD, the emperor ordered the cessation of persecution and made Christianity a legal religion, albeit one among many such religions. Around 313 AD there was a momentous event that brought about a complete change in the status of Christianity. With the conversion of the emperor Constantine, Christianity became the religion of the imperial establishment. This new imperial status of the Christian faith meant that its unity and policies were not only of significance to the various Christian communities but now also a matter of significance to the state. Various existing religious and philosophical frameworks were examined to see if they could be adapted in the quest for the best way of making sense of Jesus without reducing him in status to just another religious figure. However, the church came to realize that no existing analogy or model was good enough to meet its needs and resolve the many issues regarding Jesus and his relationship with God:

- Was Jesus the Christ a creature created by God?
- If Jesus the Christ is not divine it would not be proper to worship him.
- However, if Jesus the Christ is divine then he can disclose both what God is like and what God wants.
- If he was divine, was there a time before he existed?
- Only God can save/redeem as no creature can redeem another creature.

Once theologians had rejected the idea that Jesus was human they were left with the problem of having two distinct gods, the creator and Jesus the Christ. This is further complicated by the insistence that God is constant, does not change, cannot be manipulated, and has always existed. Hence Jesus the Christ must have always existed. When we add the idea of the Holy Spirit we are now considering three gods.

## The Quest to Understand

- Father: the creator.
- Son: the savior.
- Spirit: the means by which we are transformed and renewed.

Although it had been recognized for many years that it was important to develop and agree a basic set of doctrines that would define the essence of the Christian faith, it was not until May 325 AD that Emperor Constantine summoned all the bishops to a council in Nicaea (now Iznik in Turkey) to end the various interpretations and agree on a common story. Constantine declared that it was vital for the unity of the empire that they agreed on a single understanding for the imperial religion (but remember it was not the only religion within the empire). He also aligned the structure of the church with that of the state. There were a total of seven of these ecumenical councils held in Turkey. At the second council, in 381 AD, agreement was reached on a statement on Christian belief known as the Nicene Creed.

> I belive in one God the Father Almighty, Maker of heaven and earth, And of all things visible and invisible:
> And in one Lord Jesus Christ, the only-begotten Son of God, Begotten of His Father before all worlds, God of God, Light of Light; Very God of very God, Begotten, not made, being of one substance with the Father, By whom all things were made: Who for us men, and for our salvation, came down from heaven, and was incarnate[1] by the holy Ghost of the Virgin Mary, And was made man, And was crucified also for us under Pontius Pilate. He suffered and was buried, And the third day he rose again according to the Scriptures, And ascended into heaven, And sitteth on the right hand of the Father. And he shall come again with glory to judge both the quick and the dead: Whose Kingdom shall have no end.
> And I believe in the holy Ghost, the Lord and Giver of Life, Who proceedeth from the Father and the Son, Who with the Father and the Son together is worshiped

---

1. Incarnation, deriving from the Latin term for "flesh," summarizes the belief that Jesus is both divine and human.

PART II—CHRISTIANITY UNPACKED

and glorified, Who spake by the prophets. And I believe in one holy Catholick and Apostolick Church. I acknowledge one baptism for the remission of sins, And I look for the Resurrection of the dead, And the life of the world to come. Amen.[2]

The Roman emperor Theodosius required that all Christian churches preached the approved faith correctly by following the creeds and thus avoid heresy. Churches have continued to the present day in their use of the creeds for the following purposes:

1. To promote unity.
2. To resolve heresy.
3. For the individual assertion of belief.
4. As part of an acceptance of membership of the church.
5. To provide continuity for new converts and the next generation.

By 391 AD Emperor Theodosius had also closed all pagan temples and stopped their practice of animal sacrifices.

The fourth council in 451 AD at Chalcedon marked the end of centuries of theological debate by finally producing a definition of the nature of Jesus the Christ. The term Chalcedonian Definition is often used to refer to the fundamental idea of the two natures of Christ. It must be noted, however, that, provided it was recognized that Jesus was both truly divine and truly human, understanding how this could possibly be so was not of fundamental importance.

> Therefore, following the holy fathers, we all with one accord teach men to acknowledge one and the same Son, our Lord Jesus Christ, at once complete in Godhead and complete in manhood, truly God and truly man, consisting also of a reasonable soul and body; of one substance [*homoousios*] with the Father as regards his Godhead, and at the same time of one substance with us as regards his manhood; like us in all respects, apart from sin; as regards his Godhead, begotten of the Father before

2. Cranmer, *Book of Common Prayer*.

## The Quest to Understand

the ages, but yet as regards his manhood begotten, for us men and for our salvation, of Mary the Virgin, the God-bearer [theotokos]; one and the same Christ, Son, Lord, Only-begotten, recognized in two natures, without confusion, without change, without division, without separation; the distinction of natures being in no way annulled by the union, but rather the characteristics of each nature being preserved and coming together to form one person and subsistence [hypostasis], not as parted or separated into two persons, but one and the same Son and Only-begotten God the Word, Lord Jesus Christ; even as the prophets from earliest times spoke of him, and our Lord Jesus Christ himself taught us, and the creed of the fathers has handed down to us.[3]

*The concepts of The Trinity and the dual nature of Jesus (truly divine and truly human) were developed by the church during the fourth and fifth centuries.*

At the heart of imperial politics the official nature of Christianity meant that the position of Christ and the role of the emperor were now closely aligned. This process continued such that Christ became elevated to be seen as a cosmic emperor. The depiction of Christ became more of a warrior king who defeated his enemies and thus kings within Christendom declared that they received their own authority directly from this warrior Christ.

*This image and status of Jesus of Nazareth was already far removed from someone who suffered a Roman execution for criminals on the outskirts of Jerusalem.*

As the Roman Empire began to decline Arianism once again grew in popularity but eventually the Nicene Creed version of Christ succeeded in becoming the agreed, official version. However, far from promoting unity, the editing of the Nicene Creed by the Western Church, such that it stated that the Holy Spirit proceeds from both the Father *and* the Son, was the cause for the

---

3. Chalcedon Formula.

"Great Schism" of 1054 AD, which was when Pope Leo IX and Patriarch Michael I of the Eastern Church excommunicated each other.

## Of Death and Salvation: The Middle Ages

The five-hundred-year period from mid-eleventh century to mid-sixteenth century are known as the Middle Ages, when the discussions focused on the meaning of the crucifixion and just how Jesus the Christ brought salvation to his believers. Unlike earlier debates about the identity of Jesus, which were concluded at the ecumenical councils, there was no agreed statement on the nature of salvation so the following paragraphs summarize some of the arguments surrounding the need for salvation, the meaning of salvation, and how we gain salvation.

A central theme of the Christian message is that the death and resurrection of Jesus the Christ provides humanity with the means to be transformed and come close to God. The New Testament declares that God has given us a victory through the resurrection of Jesus the Christ and defeated sin. It speaks of Jesus giving his life as a ransom for sinners. Now a ransom has to be paid to someone but it could not be paid to God as God would not hold sinners to ransom; therefore it had to be the devil. How had the crucifixion of Jesus the Christ reconciled us to God and appeased God's righteous anger at human sin? As people struggled to explain the purpose of the crucifixion they had turned to the familiar language of sacrifice as both Jews and pagans had practiced animal sacrifices. The New Testament, drawing on Old Testament imagery and expectations, presents Jesus the Christ's death as the ultimate and perfect sacrifice. It was able to accomplish the once-and-forever atonement for human sin that the animal sacrifices of the Old Testament could not. However, St. Paul preached that we are saved by our faith in the resurrected Jesus the Christ and not by our works. For St. Paul salvation brought the freedom to grow into the likeness of God, to live the life that the resurrection had made possible.

## The Quest to Understand

The debates and questions around salvation continued to ebb and flow during the Middle Ages and if it appears confused then that is a good indication of how humankind has struggled to make sense of something that looks like a defeat. (So if you have difficulty in following these discussions then you are in good company.)

In the Eastern churches the crucifixion was seen as a victory over the hidden and malign spirits that tyrannized human beings:

- Humanity was held captive by the powers of sin, death, and the devil.

- God's rescue or liberation of humanity was achieved through the confrontation and disarming of these evil spirits through the death and resurrection of Jesus.

However, in Western churches the basic thought was that he died in place of humanity:

- God cannot restore us to fellowship with him without first dealing with human sin.

- A payment must be made for the offense of human sin.

- That payment had to be equivalent to the weight of human sin.

- The Son of God became incarnate and would possess both the human obligation to pay and the divine ability to pay the huge price necessary for redemption.

Despite the somewhat brief and simple history that I have given above it should be clearly understood that both concepts of a glorious victory and of a terrible sacrifice existed alongside each other for some centuries. Intellectual debate was one of the major characteristics of the Middle Ages with scholars drawing on the scriptures and on classical Greek philosophy.

## Of a Fractured Church: The Reformation

In the 1500s life in the West was dominated by the Catholic Church, which shaped every aspect of life, and the main concern of the people was to achieve salvation and avoid eternal damnation. The majority of the population believed in the teachings of the church, respected their priests, and took a great deal of comfort from its services, support, and activities. It was taught that the bread and wine of the Eucharist were literally transformed into the body and blood of Jesus the Christ. (The technical term is transubstantiation.) However, the masses were held in Latin, which very few people understood. Purgatory was thought to be an intermediate state between heaven and hell where bad deeds were purged before entry into heaven was granted. To raise money the church sold indulgences by which the time spent in purgatory could be reduced by a cash payment. To raise even more money this was extended so that you could buy indulgences for your already deceased relatives, with the catchy slogan attributed to John Tetzel (1465–1519), "As soon as the coin in coffers rings the soul from purgatory springs."

Leading thinkers of the sixteenth century began to question excesses in the church and various developments in beliefs and practices, such as the sale of indulgences, which seemed contrary to the true message of Christianity. Martin Luther and John Calvin are probably the two most well-known campaigners for reform within the Catholic Church. Whilst some reformers protested about corruption in the life of the church, Martin Luther, who was a pastor and professor at the University of Wittenberg, was more concerned about the distortion of the theology of the Christian faith. He despised how the church had made God's gift of grace dependent upon a complex system of indulgences and good works. In his famous Ninety-Five Theses, he claimed that the pope had no authority over purgatory and that the Catholic Church's doctrine of the saints was not based on the gospels. His intention was to force the Catholic Church to reform but it was not prepared to engage in any such debate, so in 1521 AD Luther was excommunicated. What had begun as an internal reform movement became a split from the Catholic Church and the start of numerous separate Protestant and Reformed churches across the Western world.

Although both Luther and Calvin were happy to continue with the medieval doctrines, which were based on the creeds of

## The Quest to Understand

the late Roman Empire, there were many others who called for a radical re-examination of faith. The Reformation's emphasis on a personal relationship with God and with individuals being free to interpret the scriptures as they wished resulted in some interpretations that were far removed from the Christianity taught by the Catholic Church. For example, I have previously mentioned Servetus, a Spanish theologian who developed an understanding of Jesus that was not based on the Trinity. Many of Servetus' ideas could be considered ahead of their time in that they envisaged God as the essence of all things and revealed in all things. While visiting Geneva Servetus was arrested and on the 27th of October 1553 he was burned at the stake outside Geneva. The Socinians were another example of a major group who believed that Christ was not God but was empowered by the Holy Spirit.

The printing press, a radicle new invention, facilitated the spread of books and pamphlets in the local language and this fueled the Reformation. Luther translated the Bible from Latin into German so that more people could have access. William Tyndale heard what Luther was doing and translated the Bible into English producing what many believe to be the most important book ever published.

In England the Reformation's roots were both political and religious. Pope Clement VII refused to grant King Henry VIII an annulment of his marriage, which led to the split from the Catholic Church and, in 1534 AD, the establishment of the Anglican Church with the king as the supreme head. This dramatic restructuring of the church in England allowed for a fundamental change in how worship was experienced by the general public with the preparation of a liturgy in English. Cranmer, who had originally been employed to collect evidence to support the case for Henry VIII's divorce, wrote the *Book of Common Prayer*, a copy of which was placed in every church in England. In Scotland, John Knox, who had lived in Geneva and was greatly influenced by John Calvin, led the establishment of Presbyterianism, which helped smooth the way for the eventual union of Scotland and England.

The Reformation spread to so many other European countries during the sixteenth century that by mid-century the ideas of Martin Luther dominated churches in Northern Europe. In Eastern Europe, where the kings were weak, there were even more radical versions of Protestantism established. In Spain and Italy, however, the pope retained his authority and Protestantism never gained a strong foothold in those parts of Europe.

If the Reformation of the sixteenth and seventeenth centuries comprised a dynamic but divisive time for Christianity, the eighteenth century was a period when a very different approach was taken to the understanding of the faith.

## Of Science and Rationalism: The Enlightenment

The Enlightenment was a formative period in the modern history in all areas of Western thought and culture; it began in the 1650s and ran throughout the eighteenth century. It had a huge impact on science, philosophy, the understanding of society, politics, and sparked a revolution in the way we thought about God, the Bible, and ourselves.

The Reformation had ended the dominance of the Roman Catholic Church, allowing for radically different ideas about faith to be explored during the Enlightenment period, including the search for the historical Jesus and a more critical and rational reading of the New Testament. Some scholars dismissed all the miraculous events as inventions of the early church, constructed so that Jesus fulfilled all the Jewish criteria in order to be declared as the Messiah. Others rejected this approach, arguing that this search for the historical Jesus was futile and the way forward was to take a leap of faith in Christ as the incarnate savior who saved humankind from sin through his death and resurrection. Some people argued to accept the existence of God and the afterlife but to reject the intricacies of Christian theology. Human aspirations, they believed, should not be centered on the next life, but rather on the means of improving this life, where worldly happiness was placed before religious salvation.

In the discussions that took place during the Enlightenment we can detect the basis for today's liberal Christian theology and the debates that are still ongoing. Perhaps, as theology deals with something that cannot be scientifically proven, it is inevitable that humankind will always struggle to find the answers.

## Of World Wars and Charisma: Modern Times

The people of the twentieth century were traumatized by the horrors of two world wars that made many question the belief in a merciful God. The contrast in the world between the beauty of creation and the horror of war inspired some to seek for a new understanding of God whilst others ceased to believe in God altogether. It was a period that produced some of the greatest advances in Western thinking about God and our understanding of Christianity. A very few of those that led this advance are mentioned below:

Rudolf Karl Bultmann (1884–1976): believed that Jesus the Christ's resurrection was not an actual event but a statement of faith that your old self needed to metaphorically die and be reborn in order to experience the full glory of the Christian faith.

Dietrich Bonhoeffer (1906–1945): one of the leading theological thinkers of the twentieth century, who opposed the Nazis so that they first imprisoned him and eventually hanged him.

Jürgen Moltmann (b. 1926): much of Bonhoeffer's work was continued by Moltmann, who argued for the liberation from evil via belief in the crucifixion and resurrection of Jesus the Christ.

John Robinson (1919–1983): an Anglican bishop who in 1963 published a short book entitled *Honest to God*, which for many people redefined the way we think about God and how God works.

In contrast to these intellectual searches for greater theological understanding there were those who advocated a faith led by an emotional involvement with God and the Holy Spirit. This movement, known as Charismatic Christianity, emphasizes the work of the Holy Spirit in the life of a believer and finds evidence of God working through miracles and other signs and wonders. Some criticize this movement for being overly emotional but from the 1960s it began to spread through a number of the mainstream denominations, both Protestant and Catholic. This movement now represents the fastest-growing element within Christianity today and approximately 25 percent of the Christian population attends such churches. Charismatic Christians tend to be traditional in their outlook, having a Bible-based theology and staying with the creeds of mainstream Christianity.

Today we have countless brands of Christianity. Not only is there the Roman Catholic Church and the Eastern Orthodox Church, but there is the Anglican Church, the Baptist church, the Methodists, the United Reformed Churches, the Plymouth Brethren, the Salvation Army, the Quakers, the Jehovah's witnesses, etc., etc., etc. It looks as if everyone is free to start their own church, but within it they can be as intolerant of those in other churches as they like. Those who are certain they know the truth assert that people can only be saved by believing correct doctrines; they think that there are some sets of doctrines that need to be defined as correct by some authority, which can then exclude and condemn contrary views as heretical. The irony of all this is that the Protestant movement exists because it asserted the right of dissent, the importance of free personal decision, and the rejection of a dogmatic teaching authority. It gave rise to the ability for all to have access to the Bible in their own language and encouraged debate.

*The battle lines continue to divide more liberal and conservative Christians.*

Another feature of recent years is the rise of liberation theology, which promotes the political and social elimination of the causes of poverty, the emancipation of the poor and the marginalized, together with liberation from selfishness and sin. The most important figure in liberation theology is said to be a Peruvian Dominican monk called Gutierrez. Along with liberation theology there is also the promotion of feminist theology, the quest for equal regard for both women and men. Here Jesus was regarded as revolutionary in his dealings with women because he did not treat them as second-class but treated all humanity as equally important. Today it can seem as though the first-century Jewish prophet Jesus of Nazareth has been replaced by a Jesus who has become a brand name and a bandwagon to drive almost any social reform.

## Summarizing an Unpacked Christianity

Over the previous chapters we have looked at approximately four thousand years in the development of Christianity; if it appears like an ordered and logical process then that is just a mirage as it was most likely a messy, chaotic process with phases and ideas overlapping and clashing. That is the way of most developments in human society no matter how they appear in the history books. The characters involved have long gone and so we are left with scraps of information, and probably much misinformation, with which to reconstruct a story that fits with what we can deduce. Much of it is speculation and not scientifically provable facts. However, I have tried to present, in a very brief and hopefully digestible form, the story of Christianity but it should be understood that some people will disagree with most of it and most people will disagree with some of it. I freely admit that I do not belong to the theological club of academics and clerics but this fact gives me a freedom to tell the truth as I see it, although I would recommend that you seek the opinions of others before you accept anything that I have said as the truth.

In summary, the story of Christianity started about four thousand years ago when a shepherd later known as Abraham is acknowledged as introducing the concept of one supreme God (monotheism). This is the God that became recognized by both Christianity and Islam as well as being the God of Judaism. By the time of Jesus of Nazareth the Jewish people lived under Roman oppression in a whirlpool of conflicting beliefs in gods and demons that controlled every aspect of life. The Jews were anticipating the arrival of their promised Messiah, who would herald the destruction of the world as it was and introduce a new era where the will of their God would dominate life on earth and heaven. Jesus brought a message about the imminent arrival of the kingdom of God and urged all Jews to prepare. After the absolutely devastating events of the crucifixion and the non-arrival of a new kingdom the followers of Jesus regrouped in Jerusalem under the leadership of Peter and James, the brother of Jesus, and they preached the teachings of Jesus to the Jews. Meanwhile Paul of Tarsus also began to teach about faith based on the resurrection of Jesus but his teachings were not acceptable to Peter and James as he did not require observance of the Jewish law. Thus there was disharmony and disagreement on the fundamental principles of Christianity from the very beginning. With the conversion of Emperor Constantine, Christianity moved from an obscure Jewish sect to become the imperial religion with much influence, power, and bureaucracy. Creeds were developed to ensure everyone was "on message" with belief in the Trinity of the Creator, Jesus, and the Holy Spirit united in the one God. Over the years the church grew in influence and ideas evolved about how faith in Jesus could ensure salvation so that after death you would reach heaven and avoid hell.

*During long periods of history the prospect of not achieving salvation and being condemned to spend eternity in hell must have been a terrifying thought for most people.*

As it held the keys to salvation, the church and the pope wielded absolute power and some began to see the spread of corruption and greed. Thus a movement arose to reform the church, break its power, and reassert the message of salvation through faith in Jesus. There followed a Christian jihad, a holy war, where thousands were killed, many horribly. Later, during the Enlightenment, a more rational approach was taken to the teachings of the church where the scriptures were analyzed in the same way as other ancient writings. Over the past few centuries we have seen the rise of hundreds upon hundreds of Christian churches and sects all proclaiming that they know the truth. The fastest growth

## The Quest to Understand

in Christianity over recent years has been in those churches known as Charismatic, where a more emotional type of worship is followed.

*Today it seems that, for many people, seeking salvation is no longer a priority as it is felt to be more important to have a personal relationship with God and feel the love of God.*

Alongside these developments there has been an enormous amount of serious theological debate and research leading to the publication of numerous books on an updated understanding of Jesus and the Christian faith. The churches often appear reluctant to bring this research to the attention of their congregations, or perhaps those congregations are just not interested and feel more comfortable with a more traditional understanding.

I have now concluded my short review of the background and development of the Christian religion, which comprises part II of this book. In part III, I start by presenting various thoughts on the Christian faith and religion in general. Then I can feel free to let my imagination take off and speculate on God and life after death, and search for that elusive meaning to our lives.

*Part III*
---
## THOUGHTS

# 7

## THOUGHTS ON RELIGION

Part II told the story of Jesus of Nazareth and the rise of the Christian religion up to the present day. In part III, I present various information and concepts so that we can try to move forward towards answering the questions asked at the beginning of this book:

- Will your death be the end of you or is there something more?
- Is it credible to have religious belief in the twenty-first century?
- Can there be a deeper meaning to life?

Whilst remembering that this is not a religious book in the sense that there is no preaching of a faith, I do want to begin part III by talking about religion and whether there is any place for religion in today's world. However, before considering religion in general I should complete the story of Christianity by clarifying how that story may be understood in light of recent research so we can move towards deciding what is credible and what is not.

PART III—THOUGHTS

# Christianity: What Would They Have Thought?

Perhaps a fruitful exercise to start with would be to imagine what those who initiated the religion some two thousand years ago would have to say about Christianity today.

Jesus of Nazareth saw himself in the tradition of the Jewish prophets, shaking up the establishment and calling for the Jews to prepare for the coming of the kingdom of God by maintaining the covenant with God and observing the Law. I expect he would have been astonished to have, created in his name, a separate, non-Jewish religion that has often been hostile towards the Jews.

I also would expect that Peter and James of the early Jesus movement would have hoped for Judaism to have been reformed to include recognition of Jesus as the promised Messiah. Likewise, the author of the gospel according to Matthew would have advocated that what became Christianity would be much closer to Judaism.

Paul of Tarsus and the author of the gospel according to Mark might be more accepting of the separation of Christianity and Judaism but I expect they would be saddened by the fractured nature of the church today and how different understandings of the meaning of faith in the resurrection have become entrenched. A religion united in its understanding of Jesus the Christ it is not.

## Christianity: The Gospels

As already mentioned, it was several years after the execution of Jesus that the gospels were written by people who were already convinced that he was the promised Messiah and had been raised from the dead by God. As such, they were also convinced that Jesus had been transformed into a heavenly being that possessed all the powers and abilities that such beings were assumed to have. As a heavenly being Jesus would, of course, have been able to perform miracles such as walking on water and the gospel authors had no difficulty in giving such ability to the earthly Jesus so that their readers would be convinced of his special status. The performance of miracles was also used to drive home an important point, such as when a blind man was able to see just before the disciples finally understood the true nature of Jesus, i.e., their eyes were opened!

Alongside the nature miracles there are various other stories in the gospels that are there because they confirm either that Jesus fulfils the promises of the Old Testament or that his life shows his divine nature as bestowed by God. These stories include the birth narrative featuring the virgin conception. The gospel authors each provided their own interpretation of the significance of Jesus and how faith in him should be enacted. Together with the letters of Paul and Acts the gospels present a range of contradictory theological thoughts and each one gives a very biased, limited, sometimes inconsistent message on the Christian faith. They are, however, fantastically skillful works that are inspiring to many.

## Christianity: The Impact of Saint Paul

Nobody could dispute that Saint Paul has had a decisive impact on the beliefs and direction of the Christian churches. His personal conviction that Jesus had been resurrected could be considered as the single most important event in the development of Christianity. Paul put faith in the resurrection of Jesus at the heart of his theology and, in many ways, allowed that to overshadow the whole of the life, mission, and teachings of Jesus. The creeds that are said in churches are based more on the theology of Paul than the prophecy of Jesus regarding the kingdom of God. Paul opened up the availability of salvation to anybody who had faith in Jesus, thus enabling Christianity to blossom outside of its Jewish roots and, with the demise of the Jesus movement in Jerusalem, it grew and grew as a separate religion.

*Therefore it does seem reasonable to consider that Paul was, in many respects, more responsible for the Christian faith as we know it today than was Jesus.*

PART III—THOUGHTS

## Christianity: The Nature of Jesus

The following section presents thoughts regarding Jesus of Nazareth that, although they may upset some, are the nearest we can get to understanding the person who lived two thousand years ago in Israel. It may seem that we cannot say much about Jesus with complete certainty apart from the fact that he really did exist as a historical figure, but hopefully it is helpful to say more providing it is accepted that the following is based on probabilities and possibilities.

As previously stated, Jesus saw himself as a prophet in the tradition of Jewish prophets and as a teacher of wisdom. He was convinced that the kingdom of God would be realized in the very near future and he was desperate to warn the Jews to prepare themselves for the coming age that was about to dawn. This conviction was based on his passionate conviction of his closeness to the God of Israel to which he prayed and worshipped. He had such a dynamic, charismatic personality that he compelled people to listen to him, to believe that he was filled with the spirit of God, and to leave everything and follow him. He was not meek and mild but bursting with energy with an inner conviction that saw him upset many, especially the temple authorities. To present a modern-day example, imagine someone marching into the Vatican to harangue the cardinals, telling them to discard all their privileges and badges of office before repenting before God. That would require overwhelming self-belief and a disregard for the consequences. Jesus was so completely self-absorbed with his mission that he had little time for social niceties and could be off-hand and brusque with his own mother, so whilst some regarded him as eccentric others thought him insane. At times it must have been uncomfortable to be close to Jesus but his energy and charisma drew people to him and he was able to perform healings and exorcisms for those that had absolute faith in him and who would interpret reality to fit in with how the world was believed to work. His faith healings would probably not be accepted today as actual physical cures, although

## Thoughts on Religion

it is now recognized that the mind, and what you believe, does impact bodily functions.[1]

He also was a marvelous teacher of wisdom and provided groundbreaking interpretations of the Law by applying the commonsense approach of the wisdom tradition as compared to the inflexible interpretation of the Pharisees. He was a great teacher with a gift for telling stories that would both inspire his listeners but also challenge them to rethink their beliefs. They would thus be very likely to remember what he said and pass on his teaching to others. However, we must accept that memory is also reconstructive and we all tend to remember in a way that justifies ourselves and re-enforces our expectations. It seems highly likely that Jesus' teachings were aimed at preparing the Jews for the coming kingdom as he emphasized the need for living a life of righteousness with love, mercy, and humility—a very Jewish message.

Although he was a truly remarkable person, we should accept that any supernatural aspects to his story were later additions introduced once people were convinced that he was the promised Messiah. In the ancient world it was common to believe that God would know if a baby would grow up to become an important person in the world so God must somehow have been present (but *not* involved biologically) during the conception of this important person. This is sometimes referred to as the "three in a bed" concept. Conception still required a man and a woman but the important person could subsequently be referred to as a son of God. Only Luke and Matthew include a birth narrative but Paul appears clear that Jesus was fully human and only after the resurrection, once he was in the spiritual realm, could he be considered as son of God.

*Thus it does not seem credible to consider Jesus as divine during his life on earth.*

To summarize: Jesus was wholly human, not born of a virgin but conventionally conceived. Indeed he was fallible as shown by his conviction that the kingdom of God would be established

---

1. See Lipton, *Biology of Belief.*

within a generation. Overall this makes Jesus a much more realistic, relevant, and believable figure than the perfect, supernatural being with superpowers that was part God and part human. (This may be a somewhat controversial view from a conservative Christian perspective but is, I understand, not dissimilar to the Islamic view of Jesus). His remarkable life would, in my opinion, make for a fascinating film showing him as a real person living in ancient times who initiated a revolution in the way humankind thinks and lives.

We have to accept that some people were totally and absolutely convinced that he was resurrected, but that is not the same as saying that he was divine. The reports of the risen Jesus were based on various visions and emotions that were experienced. Those experiences were so intense that they completely changed people for the rest of their lives and, although many went on to endure unimaginable suffering, they remained convinced of the truth of that resurrection. Further thoughts on the possibility of experiencing visions of the dead will be presented in the chapter "Thoughts on Life and Death." For now we should just note that belief in the resurrection has become the core of the Christian faith and the teachings of Jesus have become somewhat secondary whilst his key message regarding the imminent coming of the kingdom of God has been reinterpreted and marginalized.

## Christianity: The Doctrines

The teachings of Jesus still have much to inspire us today and his mission regarding the love of God and the command to love our neighbor is as relevant to many today as it was in his time. However, we do need to move on from the Old Testament concept of a judgmental God and I shall present various thoughts regarding God in a later chapter. For now it is just important to note that the concept of a loving and merciful God who demands sacrifices of either humans or animals is bizarre.

We have already seen that Christian beliefs have been changed and developed by humankind over the centuries in order to accommodate new knowledge and ways of thinking. It could be argued that many of those beliefs need updating again as they are no longer credible and should be consigned to the past. Given the previous section on the nature of Jesus, if that is accepted as the most probable description of him and his life, then it would appear illogical to accept the doctrine of the Trinity, or any of the ideas about atonement, or that Jesus was a sacrifice to appease God for the sins of humanity.

## Christianity: The Creeds

Given the aforementioned it will come as no surprise that many have difficult in accepting several aspects of the creeds that are conventionally used in most services. There are various individuals and Christian organizations, such as Modern Church, who are trying to push for modernization of the doctrines and to revise the creeds. However, the vast majority of churches appear to be either unaware of such initiatives or perhaps are fearful and see them as dangerous and undermining the true faith.

## Christianity: Faith

It seems that many Christians have only the vaguest understanding of the theology that underpins their faith. However, it has to be accepted that many of those who study Christian theology retain a deep faith in Christianity even if they advocate changes in the way it is taught and presented by the churches. It is often asserted that the books of the Bible, although they have been written by men, were inspired by the Holy Spirit and that the developments over the last two thousand years have been similarly guided. It is perhaps a feature of the human intellect and curiosity that ideas are continually developed, refined, and updated but it is a matter of personal belief whether or not the Holy Spirit was involved. I know of many people who I admire and respect, both for their intellect and their personality, who are deeply convinced of the truth of their religion even though they cannot prove that truth. Religious belief has to be fundamentally a matter of faith.

I would warn, however, against a faith that is based on the idea that there is a God who is there to grant your wishes and answer your prayers, as I have known people whose faith comes crashing down when injustice strikes them or their loved ones and it seems that God has ignored their pleas for justice.

## Christianity: The Church

It is without doubt that the Christian churches do much good work in many parts of the world, living by the words of Jesus by tending to the poor, the downtrodden and the sick.

The Christian churches are, however, fragmented; they cannot agree on the interpretation of the Bible and give conflicting and confusing messages on many subjects. It seems reasonable to argue that they would gain much more than they stand to lose if they embraced the work done in analyzing the New Testament documents and engaged in a constructive dialogue on the outcome. To the establishment it may seem that the results of this analysis are often used to support the arguments that there is not a sound foundation for Christianity and the teachings of the church. It is perhaps because of this that the church has often seemed reluctant to discuss this analysis openly with their congregations with the result that much of the teachings by some of the clergy are way out of date compared to the teachings available in the more forward-thinking universities and colleges. With an educated population familiar with the latest scientific advances and historical research being the subject of television documentaries and articles in the media, this reluctance by the church appears short-sighted as what they are preaching seems more and more out of touch with reality. Better, therefore, to embrace the latest analysis of the biblical text, openly engage with the discussions and promote a faith-based interpretation. Surely it is no longer valid to credit biblical quotations directly to Jesus but it is both valid and instructive to appreciate his teachings and consider how they can influence the way we lead our lives and treat our fellow human beings.

## THOUGHTS ON RELIGION
## Beware Those Who Are Certain

Having read part II of this book you may have already concluded that there is little purpose or use for organized religion but that would be an oversimplification for there are many positive contributions that religions make in the lives of many people and their communities. However, before we can think about those positive aspects of religion we have to face up to the fact that religion has often had a bad press which seems to be fully justified. Throughout history wars have been fought and killing justified in the name of religion and it continues to be the same today. It is not just the violence and intolerance that is evident between religions; it is often just as awful, if not worse, between sects or factions of the same religion. Before those of us in the West start saying that this is mainly a problem for the rest of the world we should consider our own bloody past and our involvement in the troubles in other parts of the world. It was only a few years ago that ethnic and religious wars were being fought in Europe and it is highly probable that more atrocities will occur in the future.

Most major faiths have developed over many centuries and in various scriptures, holy writings and books they have recorded the traditions and beliefs of the faithful. In nearly all cases these writings are acknowledged as being the thoughts and understandings of men even if it is believed that those men have been guided by a deity. The major exception, perhaps, is Islam, where the text of the Qur'an is believed to have been transmitted by Allah to his messenger Muhammad. However, even in the case of Islam much human interpretation over the will of Allah has taken place during the past fourteen hundred years. Yet, despite these non-divine interpretations of the will of God, devout followers of all religions quote their ancient holy writings as if there is not the slightest doubt that they accurately state how we should behave today. Even within a religion various factions provide different interpretations but each faction appears to be absolutely certain that they, and they alone, truly understand and follow the will of God. The inevitable result is that all around the world there are people who are convinced that they know how we must live, what we must believe, and how we should act in order to comply with the commands of God. Others must either be converted to believe the same or they will be condemned to eternal damnation.

The foregoing may be an exaggeration and there are, of course, many worthy exceptions of tolerant, open-minded, sincere and devout believers in all faiths. However, all religions do seem to have the capacity to foster intolerant fundamentalists who are absolutely certain that they are right and are willing to kill anyone whom they believe threatens their beliefs. It is extremely difficult to equate the fact that nearly all religions emphasize the obligations on their followers for compassion and charity with the hatred expressed for anyone else who is different and does not share their own version of their faith. This can be a major barrier to accepting the validity of any religion as it is difficult to understand how anyone can have a positive religious faith whilst ignoring the damage that religious faith causes.

Perhaps a more positive reflection on religion is to accept that the religions are not in themselves the problem but it is us, the misguided and intolerant humans, who are the cause of the problems.

## Many Faiths but One Journey

In the past most religions were exclusive; that is, they preached that only they possessed the truth and that only the followers of their faith would achieve the desired goal, whether that be salvation, paradise, rebirth, blissful assimilation, etc. There are many today who still hold this same view and use tortuous logic to explain how their deity deals with those less fortunate souls who have not had the opportunity to follow the correct path. For example, some Christians believe that only faith in Jesus will lead to salvation and a place in heaven but also believe that God loves all of humanity and wants everyone to be saved. They thus propose that non-Christians may be actually Christians but they are just not aware of that fact. Logically this must also work the other way round, e.g., Buddhists could argue that Christians are actually Buddhists but that they are unaware of this fact.

A more logical and positive approach to multiple religions, and one that seems to make common sense, is pluralism, where all mainstream religions are accepted as equally valid and are just indicative of the varied ways available to achieve similar goals. I am not sure if various religions have arisen because of the needs of different cultures and climates or if various cultures have arisen because of the different religions. It would, however, be a wonderful development for humanity if, as we move towards a more integrated and multi-cultural world, religions could borrow and build upon the rich heritages of other religions rather than trying to demonize and eliminate each other.

## Religion in the Community

Despite all the foregoing, religion can have a positive place within society at large and within the local community. Today, the prime purpose of many people in attending their local place of worship is to find God and receive a top-up of faith; however, it seems that finding a sense of community is just as important. If those that lead the worship teach compassion and tolerance of others and are not afraid to speak against bigotry and exclusiveness, then there is much to be admired in most religions. Religions can be a cornerstone of a community, providing a sense of identity and belonging whilst delivering moral guidance and lessons on what makes for a fulfilled life. Such a positive influence helps keep the younger members grounded and can provide a buffer against the evils and dangers present in society. There is an obvious need for us all to balance the desire for wealth, power, and pleasure with an appreciation of an ethical approach to any issue and promoting the best interests of all in the community. It may be argued that a non-religious, humanist organization could fulfill such a role but it is religions that have traditionally been the provider. Few would like to see ethics and the promotion of morals to be solely the responsibility of governments.

The distribution of charity and the provision of comfort to individuals during hard times is another vital contribution of religion. Many religious groups provide food and shelter to all in need without regard to their religious, cultural, or ethnic background. Many charitable organizations have their roots in religion even if it is the charitable deeds and not the religious aspects that are foremost today. Before we move on it is worth reminding ourselves that it has been religion that has inspired many of the greatest works of art over the centuries. Throughout all civilizations our heritage of great music, paintings, architecture and sculpture are intimately linked with the religions of those civilizations.

*Throughout history religion has always been a primary inspiration for mankind and their traditions and rituals still provide a rich and colorful backdrop to our lives today.*

## Credibility

Despite religions playing a valuable part in community life and doing good (as well as bad) throughout the world I have still not provided any thoughts on whether their beliefs could be credible. That is, are there reasonable grounds to accept that they represent the truth regarding divinity and our relationship with the holy? Can they really hold the key to understanding the meaning of life? In order to find a way forward, over the next two chapters I will present some thoughts regarding the possibilities of life after death and the existence of God.

## Further Reading

If you are interested in exploring religious beliefs then, in addition to the books already mentioned, you may find the following books useful: Aslan, *No God but God*; Borg, *Jesus*; Catchpole, *Resurrection People*; D'Costa, *Theology and Religious Pluralism*; Sanders, *Paul: A Very Short Introduction*; Spong, *Jesus for the Non-Religious*; Ward, *Re-Thinking Christianity*.

# 8

## THOUGHTS ON LIFE AND DEATH

There is an old saying along the lines that there are only two things that you can be sure of in this life: death and taxes. Well it seems that the very rich can employ the cleverest accountants to avoid the taxes that most of us have to pay but even they, as yet, have not found a way to avoid death. The rich can pay for the best health care that may extend their lives and keep them in good health but sooner or later they have to face death like the rest of us. Most people at some time in their lives will have the experience of someone dying, often of someone close like a parent, but death itself is something that none of us have experienced (unless you believe in reincarnation). We may plan for a good death that is pain free and where we are surrounded by those we love, but how can we know what to expect after our death and what can we do to prepare? That is what I will be discussing in this chapter.

### Evidence of Life after Death

There are countless books and studies that purport to demonstrate that there is life after death but none of these has yet to provide verifiable evidence that is widely accepted as proof. The main categories where evidence is offered include:

PART III—THOUGHTS

- Near-death experiences (NDEs).
- Reincarnation.
- Visitations from the deceased.
- Contact with the deceased via mediums/spiritualists.

## Near-Death Experiences

There has been considerable interest in NDEs over the past few years and a consensus has emerged regarding the following stages that are characteristic:

- Out of body.
- Entering and traveling through a tunnel.
- Seeing the light.
- Entering into the light.
- Meeting a divine being.

Not all NDEs complete all the stages and the nature of the divine being appears to depend on the culture and religious background of the person having the experience (e.g., a Christian meets Jesus whilst a Jew meets an angel). There are suggestions that NDEs are more to do with the brain being starved of oxygen than any mystical explanation but it does seem that those who do have such experiences are likely to be convinced that they have had a glimpse of an afterlife.

## Reincarnation

Many Asian religions believe in reincarnation and there are reports of children in many countries (not just Asian countries) where they have confounded adults with memories of previous lives and previous families. Many of these reports may be false, but there are some where it has been claimed that the children have accurately recalled facts about a previous life that they could not have known or been told about. Personally I remain dubious but I am willing to accept that some instances may be difficult to explain away.

## Visitations

Visits from the recently deceased are most commonly experienced by those closest to the deceased but they can happen to those with a less intimate relationship. The presence of the deceased can be experienced both visually and/or aurally or just as an overwhelming sensation that they are here. Sceptics rationalize such experiences as part of the grieving process where the bereaved is seeking reassurance and hence imagines the visitation. However, recalling the principle of the quote attributed to Woody Allen, "Just because you're paranoid doesn't mean they're not out to get you," just because the bereaved wish for reassurance doesn't mean that the experience cannot be real. Again, those who experience such visitations are often fundamentally affected by the experience. It is my experience that if you gather a group of people together then, slowly, a few of those present will disclose that at some stage of their lives they have experienced an overwhelming feeling that they are in the presence of someone deceased. Various studies over the past decades have shown that such experiences are remarkably common and occur in all countries and across all cultures. These experiences usually happen within the first year of death but occasionally can happen several years later. An obvious question is whether the resurrection sightings of Jesus would fit with these more recent studies of sightings of the recently deceased as mentioned above. Certainly the stories mentioned in the gospels would fit well within the most common types of these experiences and the overwhelming feeling that the disciples had that Jesus was present with them is again a common experience of the bereaved. The experiences reported by Paul present more of a problem. He certainly had an emotional connection with Jesus prior to Damascus, even if that was of an extremely negative nature, and the lengthy delay since his death would appear unusual although not unknown.

PART III—THOUGHTS

*We have to be honest and admit that it is not always possible to determine what actually happened all those centuries ago and that sometimes human experiences are difficult to explain.*

## *Mediums/Spiritualists*

Evidence for survival provided by mediums, spiritualists, and psychics is the most difficult to consider as there is so much scope for unscrupulous people to prey on the vulnerable. However, I do accept that there are some genuine and honest people who truly believe that they can make a connection with a spiritual being. I am personally not convinced but will strive to be open-minded.

The major difficulty with much of the evidence of survival after death is that it is a personal experience that is only apparent to the person involved and is not witnessed by others, thus making verification difficult. Again, of course, there are reports of information being disclosed by the deceased that are difficult to explain in any way other than it was provided by the deceased person. Perhaps the best we can say is that survival after death is not yet proven and so we shall consider other approaches.

## What Religions Say

A belief in life after death is common to nearly all major religions, with the aspect of us that survives death being called our soul.

## *Indian and Asian Religions*

A major theme is rebirth after death as the soul progresses through various spiritual states. The soul progresses to a higher spiritual state because of good actions performed during the present life and to a lower spiritual state because of bad actions during the present life. Hindu teaching includes the indestructability of the soul that is immortal and with which former knowledge and Karma resides. Buddha, however, teaches the desire to break the cycle of rebirth by letting go of the self, or ego, and hence being absorbed into the timeless peace of Nirvana.

## *Islam*

Belief in the continuity of a life after death is fundamental to Islam. The Qur'an teaches that we are required to do certain things during our lives, whilst refraining from doing others, so that we will go to paradise and dwell there in perfect peace. No one will escape the judgement and we will all be rewarded appropriately with either paradise or eternal humiliation based on how we act during this life. There is no second chance.

## *Judaism*

Jews believe that what is important is the way we behave during this life and we should trust in God to look after our soul after death. In line with other monotheistic religions there does seem to be a tendency to look to God to compensate us in the afterlife for the suffering experienced during this life.

## *Christianity*

Jesus talks about how we should prepare for the coming of God's kingdom on earth but says little about our life after death, although the Bible refers to ascending to be with God rather than being absorbed and losing personal identity. After his crucifixion, Peter, Paul, and others had visions of Jesus that were probably of a visual and auditory hallucination type rather than a physical presence. Christianity thus developed the concept of the salvation of our souls via belief in the resurrection of Jesus. Later came the concept of purgatory, where the soul has the time and opportunity to rid itself of any imperfections so that it is suitable to enter into the presence of the perfect God.

In both Islam and Christianity it is not clear whether the resurrected bodies are completely spiritual or physical although most Christian theologians nowadays tend towards the concept of a spiritual resurrection of a transformed body.

PART III—THOUGHTS

## Pondering the Meaning of Soul

Each of us has a concept of ourselves as an individual person but it is unclear of what anybody else is thinking when they refer to their own soul or being or self. Is their own concept of themselves the same as our concept of who they are? Almost certainly not. We cannot know how other people see us unless we ask them and that is a conversation that is rarely held. So what is this soul that religions say can survive death and enter eternity? It may be easier to start by considering some terms that we all use in everyday language but that may not mean the same to everybody:

- Brain.
- Mind.
- Consciousness.

The brain is the easiest to define as it is that grey matter that resides in our head between our ears. Scientists can study the brain and watch activity within the brain as music is heard, pictures seen, and thoughts thought. The processes that are undertaken by various parts of the brain can be mapped and the impact of physical damage to the brain can be determined. However, before we convince ourselves that we are close to fully understanding how the brain works there are still aspects that can surprise us, such as personality changes resulting from damage to the brain. It also seems that damage to the brain can alter our values and attitudes whilst behavioral learning rewires the neural pathways in our brain so who we are does seem to be dependent on the health and state of our brain.

The understanding of what we mean by both mind and consciousness can be more difficult as these terms mean different things to different people and the words can often be interchanged. It seems, however, to be generally accepted that consciousness is the state of being awake and aware of what is happening around us. However, there seems to be little agreement on what we mean by mind, or whether consciousness is an aspect of the mind, or whether the mind is an aspect of consciousness. For our purposes

I will consider the mind to be that process of thinking and recalling memories whilst consciousness is the mind together with the concept of self. That may also serve as the definition for the soul.

The next aspect to be pondered is whether the soul as defined above can exist without our physical bodies and, in particular, without our brains. Given that we know that some aspect of our self can be altered by damage to the brain, it would appear that our soul is firmly bounded by our bodies whilst we are alive. However, that is not the same as saying that upon the demise of our bodies our souls are destroyed as if there is no possibility that it can survive outside of our bodies. Whilst I am typing these words into my computer a copy is being stored automatically in what is called a cloud. I understand that this cloud is in fact a huge computer storage facility somewhere on earth but exactly how the data is transferred from my computer to this cloud without any physical contact or action is beyond my understanding. Now I am aware that, although it seems like magic to me, any competent student of such matters would completely understand what is happening and may even attempt to explain it to me. It is thus not magic but just how the technology works. When this computer develops a fault and no longer works (dies) I should be able to buy another computer (probably a better model) and download these exact words from the cloud onto this new computer and carry on writing this book. Is it thus possible that our souls could also be restored after our death?

## Pondering Death

Before I retired from work I read several books about what to expect and how best to prepare for my life after work. Many of these books were written by experts who had studied the process of retiring, the impact on both the person retiring and their family, the characteristics of a good retirement, and how best to prepare to maximize the possibility of enjoying such a good retirement. Some of the books were written by those who had retired themselves and they described their own experiences and gave advice on what

## PART III — THOUGHTS

to expect. Having read these books, I made my own decisions on what advice to follow and what to ignore but at least I felt that I was prepared for my retirement and could relax and look forward positively to what was to come.

There are many milestones in our lives for which we can prepare, or trust that others prepare for on our behalf, i.e., if we are too young or incapable. These milestones may include some of the following:

- Birth.
- Starting school.
- Starting work.
- Marriage.
- Raising children.
- Retirement.

There is a great deal of advice and experience available on all the above to make these milestones less traumatic than may be feared and death could be considered as just another one of these milestones for which we need to prepare. A quick search on the Internet does indeed find several books written so that we may be better informed and prepared for our inevitable death. These books are not, of course, written by people who have already died and are thus describing their experiences and giving advice based on that experience. There are books available written from a religious perspective, a medical perspective, a practical perspective, or a combination of these and it may be sensible if we each read a selection and decide our own preferred way to prepare. Perhaps the most famous book about death is *The Tibetan Book of the Dead*,[1] which contains much of the Tibetan Buddhist tradition and is intended to be read aloud to the dying to help them achieve liberation from the cycle of death and rebirth. I am sure though that many people may find the thought of reading any book to prepare

---

1. Rinpoche, *Tibetan Book of the Dead*.

for their own death as very morbid and prefer to leave events to take care of themselves.

*Death is a natural event and it is a personal decision on how, or if, we prepare for it; but perhaps it is a decision that we should make and not ignore and look the other way.*

## Pondering the Afterlife

In the past death has been likened to sleep, where we remember nothing and have no concept of time passing until we are resurrected to a new life in eternity. Before we think about what this new life may be like, and what may be the possibilities, we need to consider what is meant by eternity, as the prospect of living for eternity sounds as though it has the potential to be extremely boring. If we stop looking at the clock and referring to the calendar, our personal concept of how time is passing is measured by important events in our lives. Thus those memorable events in the past such as weddings, births, and deaths of loved ones as well as holidays, great experiences, and traumatic encounters are the markers in our lives by which we measure time. Typically when we are young there are many new experiences that put down these markers and hence time passes slowly, whilst when we are old relatively few new things are happening and time passes quickly. Hence our personal concept of time passing is subjective and not controlled by the clock. Science has also determined that time is relative and the speed at which we travel impacts the rate at which we age and time passes, although the prospect of time travel remains in the realm of science fiction, at least for now. It therefore seems that when we think of eternity we should not be thinking of a very, very long time that stretches ahead for ever but rather of being outside of time as we know it.

Before returning to thoughts on the afterlife it may be useful to consider the concept of an immortal soul that exists before we are born and cannot be destroyed. Our life on earth then is just a transitory period where we can gain new experiences before returning to our more natural state in eternity. It would be conceivable that we may decide (or the decision may be taken by others) to return to earth, or another world, for another life and further experiences. This, of course, brings us closer to the Asian concepts of reincarnation. In the Western world it is more usual to think in terms of a single life followed by a single resurrection although the idea of an immortal soul can be also found.

*Given the fact that we now realize that there is much we do not understand about life and how the universe works, it would seem bizarre to dismiss any possibility of an afterlife.*

It is not inconceivable that some sort of our essence, our soul, could be restored after the demise of our bodies and continue to exist in some manner. However, whatever happens, it may well be a natural process that does not require any input from a deity and has little or nothing to do with a supreme being.

## Further Reading

If you are interested in exploring ideas around life after death then, in addition to the books already mentioned, you may find the following books useful: Alexander, *Proof of Heaven*; Cohn-Sherbok and Lewis, *Beyond Death*; Moltmann, *In the End—The Beginning*; Newton, *Journey of Souls*; White, *Life Beyond Death*.

# 9

## THOUGHTS ON GOD

In this chapter I wish to talk about what may be said about God and whether there is any reason to believe in the existence of a God. Perhaps the first issue that needs to be confronted is that of naming. Whether you refer to your deity as God, Allah, YHWH, Supreme Being, the Cosmic Consciousness, Vishnu, Jupiter, the Other, the Ground of Being, etc. is more than a matter of culture; it also infers some qualities. Our trout may be restricted in its ability to contemplate the nature of humans by blowing bubbles (and perhaps also by particular movements) but we are also restricted in our ability to contemplate the nature of the divine by human language (and perhaps also by art). There are many unique languages on earth and each of them may have particular advantages and disadvantages when talking about divinity but that is not the main concern. To many people our search for a deity is a search for that which is beyond our ability to comprehend and hence it is a search for something that is beyond the ability of human language to describe. However, to stop at this point would feel like failure and like we are giving up before really trying so I will proceed no matter how difficult and frustrating that may prove to be.

For the rest of this chapter I shall refer to the deity as God as this tends to be the most widely used term in the English language.

PART III—THOUGHTS

Before we proceed too far I should like to redefine the meaning of theology from the study of God to thoughts about God as we cannot weigh, measure, or quantify God in a scientific laboratory. In line with the fundamental premise of this book we should beware of those who are certain that God exists and those who are equally certain that there is no such thing as God. Many popular books on religion purport to know all about God and include sayings such as "God's purpose is . . . ," "God loves you," and "God wants you to . . ." Other books state that there is no such thing as God and that all religion is a human-made fantasy. I find myself almost yelling at these statements in frustration: How do you know? How can you be so certain?

## The Nature of God

Over the centuries many arguments have been put forward attempting to prove that there is a God but they have all proved inadequate so perhaps we should start with a different question: If there is a God, what would the nature of that God be? Maybe we can find some useful insights in the descriptions of God used by various religions.

The nature of the Jewish God is provided in the Old Testament: "The Lord, the Lord, a God merciful and gracious, slow to anger, and abounding in steadfast love and faithfulness, keeping steadfast love for the thousandth generation, forgiving iniquity and transgression and sin, yet by no means clearing the guilty, but visiting the iniquity of the parents upon the children and the children's children, to the third and the fourth generation."[1] However, it should be noted that the understanding of God by the Jews was subject to debate and change over the centuries. The concept of God as being a judgmental divinity may have been a statement of the obvious during times when life was precarious and there was no better explanation for when natural disasters struck and wreaked havoc, disease was rife, and life was hard and, all too often, short.

1. Exod 34:6–7.

It is easy to understand why the cry was:

- Why is life like this?
- What have I done to deserve this?
- Why is God punishing me?

The answer from the priests may have been:

- Because he has judged you and found you wanting.
- Because of your sins.
- Because of your evil thoughts and deeds.

As Christianity developed people became less comfortable with this portrayal of God and moved towards a portrayal of a more personal, loving God. However, if we are to consider the Christian view of the nature of God then we have to face up to the ideas around how salvation is achieved and especially the theories of atonement. Many believe that the crucifixion and subsequent resurrection was the ultimate act of atonement for human sins and was the primary purpose for the coming of Jesus. So do we accept that this loving God required human sacrifice in order to be gracious and forgiving towards humanity? That God was powerless to find another way to atone for human sin and hence had to engineer a set of events that led to the death of his son, and not just any death but an absolutely awful kind of death? This implies that the Christian God is either cruel or not as powerful as supposed.

Why, if the main purpose of his life was to be his death, does Jesus not concentrate on his own fate during his teachings but instead has a completely different core message focusing on the coming kingdom? The gospel references to giving his life as a ransom are most likely to have been later insertions and the words of the Eucharist need to be understood within the context of Jewish tradition, where the sharing of bread is a way of identifying with the participant. The idea of a God who is a harsh judge and who can also be cruel has undoubtedly led to an enormous amount of anxiety over thousands of years with the overarching motivation for countless lives being the need to be found not guilty of sin at the Last Judgement. This has done much spiritual damage and poisoned the concept of God across much of the earth. More modern ideas center around a loving God, where judgement has become more like an appraisal of the life on earth when lessons can be learnt on how to improve. The concept of hell is seen as a rejection of God so that union with God is never achieved. However, I am in danger of straying into a discussion of what can be said about what may happen after death and that was the subject of the previous chapter so I shall move on to discuss what other religions say about the nature of God.

The theme of judgement followed by an appropriate reward or punishment is quite common. Perhaps this should not be that surprising as concepts of the divine were not developed in isolation in the ancient world but spread between cultures including Egypt, China, and the Middle East. There are, however, some different, more spiritually based concepts, such as can be found in Buddhism, that reject worship of a supreme God but teach about a wider consciousness in which there is no sense of individual self. Similarly, in some Hindu and Indian traditions there is not a supreme being but a blissful, peaceful intelligence that is the timeless, inner nature of all reality.

In order to move on we shall now look at concepts of God from a completely different starting point.

## The Mysterious Cosmos

Not many years ago it seemed that advances in scientific knowledge would soon provide a comprehensive understanding of how the universe originated and worked. It was apparent that Newtonian mechanics provided a reasonable explanation of how things behaved on earth, which was good enough for everyday purposes, but Einstein came up with a better explanation for when we considered the whole cosmos. Then all our confidence in our human ability to explain and understand, as each generation built on the store of human knowledge, began to look rather fragile. It was already speculated that the laws of nature probably broke down in the vicinity of black holes but then the Hubble Space Telescope provided measurements that showed that the universe was expanding at an accelerating rate. This was exactly the opposite of what was expected as it was thought that, with all the matter in the universe, the forces of gravity would be slowing the expansion and eventually stopping and reversing the process.

It is now recognized that we just have no explanation of what is going on, so the concept of dark energy and dark matter has been introduced to at least provide names for what we cannot detect. By applying these to the observations of the universe, scientists have calculated that the universe is made up of approximately 68 percent dark energy, 27 percent dark matter, and just 5 percent of what we always had assumed was normal matter that we can observe. There are several theories about what dark energy and dark matter may be but none of these has yet been generally accepted let alone proven. They may be a yet unrecognized property of what we had assumed was just empty space—which may be anything but empty.

In August 2012 a BBC television program in the scientific *Horizon* series looked at attempts to measure the size of the universe.

- The answer was that the universe is infinite!
- And it is expanding!
- And there may be an infinite number of universes!

All in all, our confidence that science would provide all the answers, so that there was no longer any need to invoke God, looks somewhat premature.

Maybe we need an updated concept of God that is at least compatible with our current understanding of the universe, which is thought to be around 13.8 billion years old. When Jesus of Nazareth was born the Jews believed that the earth was about four thousand years old, the earth was the center of the universe, and the people of Israel were God's chosen people on earth. We have moved a long way from that understanding to recognize that the earth is a tiny spec in an insignificant galaxy and, if there is a God, we have to wonder why God would devote any effort for such a minor player in the vastness of space.

## All in God

Up to now it has proven to be fruitless to try and prove that God exists or does not exist so perhaps a better way forward is to look for an understanding of what a God may be like that is compatible with our current understanding of the universe and our experience of life on earth. Well, God would not be an old man with a long white beard but with a surprisingly youthful and muscular body and I am also fairly sure that God is not human, male or female, a creature, or indeed any sort of being that we can imagine. What we have to do is forget our childhood images of God and start afresh and here I am grateful to the Reverend Doctor Michael Brierley for introducing me to the concept of panentheism, which just means "all in God" but for some reason is written in Greek. It is the position that God is greater than the universe, that the universe is in God, that God permeates every part of nature, is part of nature, extends beyond nature, and is also distinct from it.

There are three fundamental premises:

1. God is not separate from the cosmos.
2. God is, in some sense, affected by the cosmos.
3. God is more than the cosmos.

God is not a separate being with a separate existence. God is not "out there."

The term panentheism was first coined in the nineteenth century and, as is the way of such things, has been analyzed and complicated by theologians. However, I would prefer to consider the broad concept and not get lost in intricate debates around the details. Although panentheism has not been adopted by major religions, elements of it can be seen in the various descriptions of God in nearly every religion, especially where the deity is described as both all-powerful and intimately involved in worldly affairs and the lives of all creatures. Hence acceptance of panentheism is gaining ground as it seems to offer a way of overcoming the difficulties that people have today with more traditional models of God.

Many Christians may tolerate the more flexible liberal views about Jesus but reject any similar approach when it comes to the nature of God. There will be those who hold that God is wholly good and never changing and have a problem accepting the concept that the universe is in God as this has to include the bad and evil things as well as the good. Some panentheists counter this by arguing that they believe in an all-encompassing and fully perfect God whilst recognizing the reality of the freedom of individuals to choose good or evil even if that is within God. God will feel and experience it deeply so God cannot be unchanging and unaffected but the essence of God will not be changed.

If there is a God then panentheism seems to provide the best model around that is compatible with what we know and experience, thus uniting our intellects and our hearts.

## Experiences and Communications

Religious experiences appear to be a worldwide phenomenon combining a sense of awe at the infinity of the universe with a feeling of the divine presence, of an unseen power, followed by an overwhelming sense of peace. The obvious difficulty the rest of us have with the experiences of others is the internal, personal nature of such happenings and hence the inability to check and verify. It is also interesting that people will describe such an experience in the terms of their particular faith and/or culture. Hence Catholics speak of Mary, whilst Jews and Buddhists may experience a vision of an angel. However, it does seem that experiences of contact with the divine are a common and undeniable reality for many people across the world. They can also have a profound impact on the person involved and completely alter their life and beliefs so we must take these experiences seriously and with respect. Having accepted that fact, it should be noted that if the panentheistic model of God is correct, then the concerns of God may encompass many sentient life forms across the universe and not just humans.

## PART III—THOUGHTS

If for now we accept the reality of God, then the next questions will be around how that God influences our lives and how we can communicate. It may well be that the nature of God is loving and good but that this God does not actively interfere in our affairs. If this is the case there are reasonable questions to be asked regarding the validity of the prayers of intercession that are found in many Christian churches. It is often difficult to understand why God should be expected to give preference to someone just because they have been the subject of our prayer. For example, if there are two men suffering from cancer, one an elderly man who is a pillar of the local church whilst the other is a younger family man who is just as honest, loving and charitable but is not actively involved with any faith, should God favor the older man because his church includes him in their prayers of intercession?

In the bibliography that can be found at the end of this book I have included the novel *Silence* by the Japanese author Shusaku Endo. It is set in the seventeenth century, when a Jesuit priest goes to Japan, where Christianity has been banned and anyone accused of being a Christian has to publically renounce the faith or face horrendous torture and death. The priest is eventually captured by the authorities and has to watch while peasants are brutally murdered in an attempt to force him to renounce. Despite all the agonizing and prayers there is no intervention by God, only silence, so eventually the priest does renounce his faith. Perhaps God shares this suffering and perhaps his love can be felt, but he does not intercede. Martin Scorsese is an admirer of the novel and has made it into a film; it is very much worth watching and, although not a joyful watch, it will make you think about the nature of God.

If God does not interfere then that God is also not responsible for any of the bad things that happen such as natural disasters, diseases, plagues and famines. God may experience the suffering but that is not the same as saying that God is responsible for that suffering or can change the causes of that suffering. What, then, you may well ask, is the point of trying to communicate with this non-interfering God? Perhaps we can experience emotional peace and comfort whilst being offered guidance on how we can act within our own lives, under our own free will, to help others and to pursue our personal development and happiness.

If there is a God with whom we can communicate, then it would seem that a reasonable assumption is that there are some people who have a greater natural aptitude for communicating with the divine than the majority of us. In every field of human activity and endeavor there are always those who are more naturally gifted no matter how hard others may strive to succeed. It may be that the prophets and mystics are such gifted people, even if they do not always correctly interpret the communications they receive from the divine. For the rest of us it would seem that meditation as taught by most Asian religions may be a good way forward. For Christians it may feel more acceptable to follow the teachings of John Main (1926–1982), a Benedictine monk who championed the practice of Christian meditation as a tradition rooted in the teachings of Jesus. In the bibliography you will find details of his manual for Christian meditation, titled *Word into Silence*, and the last time I looked there were also videos freely available on the Internet of John Main explaining the techniques and practice of meditation.

In this chapter I have been exploring various ways of thinking about God:

- Is there a credible concept of God?
- What is the nature of God?
- How can we experience God?

There is a saying that goes along the lines of: "You do not prove that God exists; you believe God exists."

*Whilst I agree that you cannot prove God exists, it seems reasonable to accept the possibility that our mysterious cosmos includes an underlying basis for life that we call God.*

In the next (and final) chapter I summarize the thoughts and beliefs regarding God, religion, and the afterlife.

## Further Reading

If you are interested in exploring further ideas about God then, in addition to the books already mentioned, you may find the following books useful: Borg, *The God We Never Knew*; and Ward, *Big Questions in Science and Religion*.

# 10

## FINAL THOUGHTS

In this final chapter I gather together some key elements from earlier chapters, conclude our pondering, and attempt to provide some answers to those three questions. Understand, however, that what any of us believes does change and evolve throughout our lives as we gain more experiences, so your beliefs now may not be the same as they were ten years ago and they are likely to be different again in ten years' time. Recognizing that personal beliefs can be changed, we should all strive to remain open to the beliefs of others, especially those in our own community.

### Back to Those Questions

Throughout this book we have been striving to provide information that can be used to form the basis for answers to three questions:

- Will your death be the end of you or is there something more?
- Is it credible to have religious belief in the twenty-first century?
- Can there be a deeper meaning to life?

PART III—THOUGHTS

The following is an attempt at answers that you may feel is inadequate or unsatisfactory but I am more than happy for you to disagree. In fact you may remember that my aim in writing this book was to help you to find your own answers rather than to persuade you to agree with me.

## The Afterlife

I gave some thoughts regarding God earlier in part III but it should be understood that the existence of something called God does not automatically mean that there is an existence for us after our death on earth. There are four possible scenarios:

1. There is a God and there is some aspect of us that continues after death.
2. There is no God but there is some aspect of us that continues after death.
3. There is a God but nothing of us continues after death.
4. There is no God and nothing of us continues after death.

In chapter 8 I presented thoughts on the possibility of our personal essence, our soul, having a continuing existence after our body dies. Overall, the combination of the fact that many people have had such strong experiences of the deceased that it has convinced them of the reality of an afterlife, together with some possible explanations of how that may work, leads to the conclusion that it would be foolish to reject the possibility of an afterlife.

*So to answer the first question directly, yes, there is a possibility that some aspect of us continues to exist after our bodies die, but that is a natural process and not a gift from some deity.*

## Religious Belief

Part II comprised an analysis of the origins and development of the Christian religion and earlier on in part III I presented thoughts on what aspects of the Christian faith are believable and what aspects

## Final Thoughts

are not. The next step is to consider whether religious faith can be accepted as credible.

With an infinite and mysterious cosmos, it would be bizarre to totally dismiss the possibility of a divine reality, and if there is such a reality then panentheism seems to me to provide the most sensible model for that reality. A compatible concept of God is one full of love and compassion for all sentient beings throughout the cosmos but one that does not, or is unable to, meddle in our lives. Although such a God could not intercede in response to our prayers, there is still the possibility that there may be some personal comfort and guidance available via thoughtful, reflective prayer such as found in the practice of Christian meditation. It seems outdated to still believe in a judgmental God who punishes the wicked and rewards those who are good. The concept of an all-powerful, all-seeing God who nevertheless requires people to worship him and beg forgiveness for being the creatures he created seems to be completely illogical. Once you start thinking through how such a concept works and what it means it quickly becomes full of contradictions, several of which we have already discussed. It should be remembered that the existence or not of God does not necessarily say anything about what may await us after our life on earth has come to an end.

The resurrection of Jesus needs to be seen within the context of the widespread experiences that people have had of deceased persons throughout the world and probably have always had throughout history. The experiences of seeing, hearing, or sensing the presence of the deceased Jesus may have been overwhelming for those individuals involved but do they imply anything unique about the nature of Jesus? If it is accepted that over the generations many people have had experiences of people who are deceased, then these are more likely to be encounters with their souls in the afterlife and hence do not imply any godlike quality of the deceased. Therefore the fact that some people had experiences of Jesus after his death also does not necessarily imply that he had any godlike qualities or should be proclaimed as the risen lord.

However, we must accept that many of the wisdom teachings of Jesus of Nazareth were very insightful and are still relevant to how we can all live a fulfilled life today, so that occasionally the sermons from the pulpit can be thought provoking even if not always inspiring. Having said that, most of the beliefs of the Christian faith are human-made concepts that have been developed over the centuries since the crucifixion and that I find difficult to accept as credible.

Hence, to summarize our thoughts on the reasons and benefits of belonging to a religious organization:

- For pursuing the practice of listening to God.
- For receiving teaching on how to live a positive and fulfilling life.
- For belonging to, and supporting, the community.

*So to answer the second question directly, if you accept that there is a reasonable probability that God exists, yes, it is credible to have a religious belief in the twenty-first century.*

Note that although it may be credible to have a religious faith, it does not necessarily follow that all that your religion preaches as the truth is also credible. I would urge you to be cautious and only accept as true those aspects of your religion that have a solid foundation or where you have a deep personal faith that they are true.

If you are not currently a member of any religious group but are thinking of exploring what they could offer, then I present some of my own advice which may be of some help. For a start I would go with whatever religion best reflects your own family background and culture. I am not interested in promoting one religion over any other. Next I would try and ascertain if your local place of worship is inclusive or exclusive; that is, does it accept that there may be other paths to achieve fulfillment or does it believe that only it knows the truth? I would suggest that you keep looking until you find a place that is inclusive and welcoming. Enjoy your religion and embrace your group and community. Learn about your religion, ask questions, and resist any inclination to be swept along on a tide of emotion or to follow others just because they seem so sure of all the answers. However, we should also keep in mind that belonging to a religious organization may not change the possibility of an afterlife and nobody should be living in fear of some divine judgement.

## Pondering the Purpose of Life

Why are we so arrogant that we think we can understand how nature, including the entire universe, works? If we do come across some aspect that we do not understand then we somehow assume that, given sufficient time, we will be able to figure it out, understand and explain it. Is it just possible that there may be some things that are part of the natural order that we do not possess adequate capability to understand? It is surely better to ditch any idea of the supernatural and just accept that there are aspects of the natural order that we do not understand or even know that they exist. It seems unlikely that the trout will ever grasp the concept of a human being, so why should we assume that there is nothing that we just cannot grasp? Over the past few decades, humanity has recognized that there is far more about the cosmos that we do not understand than was previously thought.

Over billions of years the earth has evolved and changed and will continue to do so until, once again, it becomes cosmic dust. Life on earth has evolved over hundreds of thousands of years and that evolution itself has been impacted by the changes in the earth and its climate. There was a recent newspaper article that I read where the possibility was raised that Homo sapiens evolved many years earlier than previously thought, perhaps as long as five hundred thousand years ago, still an insignificantly small time within cosmic time scales. I don't know if this is likely to prove true or not but if it is then that adds weight to the theory that Homo sapiens would have lived alongside other primitive humans and interbred, hence intermixing their DNA and creating the DNA that we carry today as modern humans. That DNA has travelled on a long, long journey from the earliest life forms and the huge time that has taken raises some interesting questions, e.g., at what point along that journey did we start having a soul?

In order to survive and to become the dominant species, our ancestors would not only have had to be the fittest of our kind but also more cunning and ruthless than any other species. Perhaps we should not always be surprised when human nature seems to be skewed towards aggression and fighting rather than loving our neighbor. If we have been evolving for half a million years to become what we are today, just imagine what we may be like in another half a million years. It could be expected that we will have a vastly better understanding of the cosmos and how the laws of nature work, but will we have bred out our aggressive, selfish, and greedy natures and enhanced our sense of love, compassion, and justice? If so, then we may be close to establishing that kingdom that Jesus described.

If there is a natural process that provides for an afterlife, what is the purpose of our time on earth? If there is no God looking over our shoulder and keeping a log of our behavior to use as evidence at the time of judgement, should we just go all out to enjoy ourselves and indulge any passing urges or desires? It is often said that a life of such indulgence turns out to be unsatisfactory and ends in a search for a more meaningful and rewarding life. That may be true but is there anything about the prospect of an afterlife that should influence how we live our lives if there is no prospect of moral judgement after our death?

If our lives on earth are just a passing phase during our existence, then may be it is part of our development, an opportunity to learn. If so then it is reasonable to expect that during the afterlife we would reflect on what we have learned, what mistakes we made, and how we could improve. It would not be a very comfortable experience if we have spent our time on earth inflicting pain and hardship on others or just not bothering to help when help was needed. It is not a case of receiving punishment for being bad but more a case of having to face up to our own inadequacies and failures. The concept of self-improvement and development by reflecting on our lives has the potential to provide a meaning for our lives that is not imposed by some higher authority. It does imply that we should live a life where we are considerate of others and help those less fortunate, and also that we should live our life to the full, embracing new experiences and loving others with abandon.

The fundamental principles for living a good life that most would agree upon seem to be:

- Show mercy and compassion.
- Go out of your way to do good, and don't do harm.
- Treat others as you would wish them to treat you.

*So to answer the third question directly; we can find meaning in our lives, without fear or anxiety about divine judgement, by striving for a good and as happy a life as possible and sharing that happiness with all.*

If it turns out after all that there is no God and no afterlife, then that is part of the natural order which we cannot change. If, however, there is a God and an afterlife, then that is great but that is also part of the natural order which we cannot change. Hence the reason for living a "good" life is not out of fear of some divine retribution if we don't, but because it is the right thing to do and will make our own life better and more fulfilled now and in any afterlife. If we do that then we can go to our death content, without worrying about what is to come.

Over the past few generations humankind has understood that events that had once been attributed to some supernatural deity (e.g., earthquakes, comets, plagues) are in fact just part of the natural order of things. Surely then it is not unreasonable to expect that this trend will continue and our understanding of nature will expand and our tendency to ascribe inexplicable events to the supernatural will diminish.

- Perhaps there is a divine existence, perhaps there is a God essence that permeates the universe, and perhaps that is just how things are.

PART III — THOUGHTS

- Perhaps there is nothing supernatural but just the natural order that we have yet to understand and recognize.
- Perhaps we are really spiritual beings who dwell in some unrecognized dimension of the universe and who just visit earth to gain new experiences.
- Perhaps our universe is within a black hole of a different universe.
- Perhaps humankind will continue to evolve over the millennia until all these questions are answered or become irrelevant.

You may consider the above as just daydreams and fantasies without any realistic probability of being found to be true. I would accept that they are purely speculation and that I cannot provide any evidence to support any of them, but I would also argue that they are no more unlikely than gods with supernatural powers walking on the earth. I have now reached the end of my pondering as far as this book is concerned, but I urge you to continue your own search to find a meaning for your own life. There are many groups and courses available that you may wish to join in order to discuss and debate various aspects of spirituality and religion. In the bibliography at the end of this book you can find details of the various books that have already been mentioned and that I have found useful during my own pondering. Many of these books are very worthy, some are inspirational, whilst others should be read with a heavy measure of skepticism.

I would recommend that you read a variety of such books, including some that are not about religion but may help trigger alternative ways of thinking about those big questions. For example, you may wish to read the English bishop John Robinson's *Honest to God*, which was written in the 1960s, and then the American cell biologist Bruce Lipton's *The Biology of Belief*, written more recently. In their very different ways these books provide ways of thinking about the nature of God as well as our own nature.

## Final Thoughts

I wish you all the best as you continue to find your own answers and work out a purpose for your life. As for myself, I shall also continue to ponder, blow bubbles and be curious.

# BIBLIOGRAPHY

Alexander, Eben. *Proof of Heaven: A Neurosurgeon's Journey into the Afterlife*. St. Ives, UK: Piatkus, 2012.
Allison, Dale C. *Resurrecting Jesus: The Earliest Christian Tradition and Its Interpreters*. London: T. & T. Clark, 2005.
Aslan, Reza. *No God but God: The Origins, Evolution and Future of Islam*. London: Arrow, 2011.
Borg, Marcus J. *The God We Never Knew: Beyond Dogmatic Religion to a More Authentic Contemporary Faith*. New York: HarperSanFrancisco, 1997.
———. *Jesus: Uncovering the Life, Teachings, and Relevance of a Religious Revolutionary*. New York: HarperCollins, 2006.
Catchpole, David. *Resurrection People: Studies in the Resurrection Narratives of the Gospels*. London: Darton, Longman and Todd, 2000.
Chalcedon Formula. http://www.anglicansonline.org/basics/chalcedon.html.
Cohn-Sherbok, Dan, and Christopher Lewis, eds. *Beyond Death: Theological & Philosophical Reflections on Life after Death*. London: Macmillan, 1995.
Cranmer, Thomas. *The Book of Common Prayer: The Texts of 1549, 1559, and 1662*. Oxford: Oxford University Press, 2013.
D'Costa, Gavin. *Theology and Religious Plurism: Signposts in Theology*. West-Sussex, UK: Wiley-Blackwell, 1986.
Endo, Shusaku. *Silence*. Translated by William Johnston. London: Picador Classic, 2015.
Lipton, Bruce. *The Biology of Belief: Unleashing the Power of Consciousness, Matter & Miracles*. London: Hay House, 2015.
Main, John. *Word into Silence: A Manual for Christian Meditation*. Norwich, UK: Canterbury, 2006.
McGrath, Alister. *Heresy: A History of Defending the Truth*. London: SPCK, 2009.
———. *Theology: The Basics*. West-Sussex, UK: Wiley-Blackwell, 2012.
Moltmann, Jürgen. *In the End—The Beginning: The Life of Hope*. Norwich, UK: SCM, 2011.

# Bibliography

Newton, Michael. *Journey of Souls: Case Studies of Life between Lives*. St. Paul, MN: Llewllyn, 2003.

Rinpoche, Guru. *The Tibetan Book of the Dead: The Great Liberation through Hearing in the Bardo*. Translated by Francesca Fremantle and Chögyam Trungpa. Boston: Shambhala, 1992.

Robinson, John. *Honest to God*. London: SCM, 1963.

Sanders, E. P. *Paul: A Very Short Introduction*. Oxford: Oxford University Press, 2001.

Smith, Douglas. *Rasputin*. London: Macmillan, 2016.

Spong, John Shelby. *Jesus for the Non-Religious*.New York: HarperOne, 2009.

Stewart, Robert B., ed. *The Resurrection of Jesus: John Dominic Crossan and N. T. Wright in Dialogue*. Minneapolis: Augsburg Fortress, 2006.

Theissen, Gerd, and Annette Merz. *The Historical Jesus: A Comprehensive Guide*. London: SCM, 1998.

Ward, Keith. *The Big Questions in Science and Religion*. West Conshohocken, PA: Templeton Foundation, 2008.

———. *Re-Thinking Christianity*. Oxford: Oneworld, 2007.

White, Vernon. *Life Beyond Death: Threads of Hope in Faith, Life & Theology*. London: Darton, Longman and Todd, 2006.

Whittock, Martyn, and Esher Whittock. *Christ: The First 2000 Years: From Holy Man to Global Brand. How Our View of Christ Has Changed across Time and Cultures*. Oxford: Lion, 2016.

"Words of the Mourner's Kaddish." http://www.mnemotrix.com/tachash/kadwords.html.

www.ingramcontent.com/pod-product-compliance
Lightning Source LLC
Chambersburg PA
CBHW050831160426
43192CB00010B/1980